# BEYOND
## THE
# SKY LIMITS

D N N S YADAV

PARTRIDGE

**To order additional copies of this book, contact**
Partridge India
000 800 919 0634 (Call Free)
+91 000 80091 90634 (Outside India)
orders.india@partridgepublishing.com

www.partridgepublishing.com/india

This book has been dedicated to

My

**Father** and **Mother**

And

The **Corona Warriors**

The Doctors, Nursing Staff, Paramedics,
Sanitary Staff, Police Personnel

Labor Communities.

For their untiring fight against Covid-19 pandemics world over.

———————————————————

# ABOUT THE BOOK

Success in your life is made synonymous to the sky limits. For those who are brave performers, sky is the limit for them. They achieve unlimited by doing tirelessly. They are unstoppable, come what may. It is your positive mindset which gives you the concentration of mind to set, pin point your life targets and the inner strength to perform. Never allow negative thoughts to enter to your mind. With the help of very easy contents of the book various facets of life struggles are identified which are commonly faced by those who have a desire to win by performing. Book suggests tips to go for certain solutions to human related life problems. Researches on human life behavior reveal that every problem has solutions provided we handle our problems with determined set of mind. Life management is very significant to ensure human success. Do not fear of depressions in your life. Depressions are good since they inspire you and make you strong from inside. Worries are inherent features of every human life. We should not expect our life without worries. You have only two options. Either you decide to live with those worries and spoil your life, or to make efforts to win over your worries and live life full with joy and happiness.

Human mind is the most powerful machine in your body system. The mind has done wonders in human achievements. So the mind does for you in your personal career success provided you have worked upon your mind very carefully at the time of supplying winners inputs to your mind. Make your mind to work for you.

Develop the habit to master your mind by supplying it positive thoughts. Your under the influence of negative thoughts is going to harm you miserably. So always be alert about choice of thoughts to your mind. Depending upon the high class quality inputs you have fed in your mind, you are going to get back, the high class quality outputs.

The contents coverage of this book is self motivating and they will help and inspire you in your struggle for career building and to get success in your life. Despite ups and downs in your life this self help book will make you strong to overcome your worries. You are born to win. Although the present Covid-19 outbreak has caused considerably painful loss of life and property world over, we would win subject to the conditions on oath that we are not going to repeat our criminal wrongs against the nature. You think, you do, and you win. Sky is the limit for you. This book will make you to think even 'Beyond the Sky Limits'. Let the success touch your feet. Your life is beautiful. Let your life be in search of peace and happiness by helping you and others as well. I wish you all the best for your life.

D. N. N. S. Yadav
June, 2020, Lucknow, INDIA

# CONTENTS

1   Work Is Religion.........................................................1

2   No Worries ...............................................................4

3   Follow Your Intuitions..............................................7

4   Fight Your Fear Out.................................................10

5   Happy State of Mind................................................13

6   Your Past Inspires ..................................................16

7   Life Has Meaning....................................................19

8   The Great People ....................................................22

9   Suffering Humanity.................................................25

10  Go For Action .........................................................28

11  Wisdom of Great Thinkers .....................................31

12  Your Peaceful Mind................................................34

13  The Trying Moments ..............................................37

14  For the Mankind .....................................................40

15  Vision for Society ...................................................43

16  Value Your Character .............................................46

17  Old Habits Die Hard ..............................................49

18  Healthy Soul ...........................................................52

19  Need Self Improvement .........................................55

20  Develop Writing Habits ..........................................58

21  You Are the Winner................................................61

22  Make Things Happen ............................................. 64

23  Welcome Adversities ..............................................67

24 The Human Touch .................................................70

25 Power of Your Thoughts .......................................73

26 Your Future Waits................................................76

27 Express Your Knowledge .....................................79

28 No Negative Thoughts .........................................82

29 Let People Explore You ........................................85

30 Attend Your Kids.................................................88

31 Do Not Blame.....................................................91

32 Have Dreams .....................................................94

33 Your Inner World................................................97

34 Do Not Fear Public Speech..................................100

35 Focus Your Targets .............................................103

36 Discover Yourself ..............................................106

37 Helping Others...................................................109

38 Practice Virtues .................................................112

39 After Your Death ...............................................115

40 Listen to Inner Voice ..........................................118

41 Master Your Thoughts.........................................121

42 Discipline Daily Pursuits.....................................124

43 Your Personal Excellence ....................................127

44 The People You Associate ....................................130

45 Reading Great Books...........................................133

46 Be Patient Listener..............................................136

47 Positive Changing...............................................139

48 Draw the Framework ..........................................142

49 Mission of your life.............................................145

50 Life Is Pleasant Story..........................................148

51 Living the Last Day ............................................151

52 Think Unique Way .............................................154

53 Potential Mind ....................................................... 157

54 Beauty of Nature.................................................... 160

55 Manage Your Time ................................................ 163

56 The Best You ........................................................ 166

57 Consistent Temper ................................................ 169

58 Forgive Others ...................................................... 172

59 Always Think Big.................................................. 175

60 Controlling your Mind........................................... 178

61 Earn Your Knowledge ........................................... 181

62 Do Not Hate.......................................................... 184

63 Welcome Critics.................................................... 187

64 For A Noble Cause................................................ 190

65 Your Personality Reflects ..................................... 193

66 Body Language...................................................... 196

67 You Are By Choice................................................ 199

68 Honesty of Words .................................................202

69 Things Right and Just............................................205

70 Manage Your Stress...............................................208

71 You Will Never Fail .............................................. 211

72 Your Optimistic Will ............................................ 214

73 World Perspectives ............................................... 217

74 Ups and Downs in Life..........................................220

75 Master Your Destiny..............................................223

76 Be Capable to Be ..................................................226

77 Friend-The Best Gifts ...........................................229

78 Future Will Be Yours.............................................232

79 Eating Habits ........................................................235

80 Setbacks Are Blessings..........................................238

81 Act Wisdom...........................................................241

82  People Thinking Negatively ...................................244
83  The Will Power...................................................247
84  Behave Your Self................................................250
85  Failures Stepping Stones.....................................253
86  Environmentally Yours.........................................256
87  Spiritual Greatness ............................................259
88  The World Awaits You.........................................262
89  Not to Lose Temper ...........................................265
90  Go For Help .......................................................268
91  Avoid Oversleeping ............................................271
92  Have Mutual Trust..............................................274
93  Understanding Life.............................................277
94  Error Is To Human..............................................280
95  Win Over Worries ..............................................283
96  Religion to Be Human.........................................286
97  Parents Real Gods.............................................289
98  Struggle Honestly .............................................292
99  No Second Innings ............................................295
100 Sky Is the Limit.................................................298
101 The Corona Warriors..........................................301

# 1

# WORK IS RELIGION

There is a very famous proverb 'work is worship'. What is the co-relationship between work and the worship? Do you worship God? Do you believe in existence of an Almighty? Whether work has anything to do with religion? What is your religion? These are very difficult questions to reply, particularly in the light of different religions prevalent in the world. It is always people's choice to practice religious faith they like to believe. Even people have the freedom to not to have faith in any religion and remain atheists. Equating your work with your daily prayers has been linked with worship as an essential part of human activities in your life. Daily worships make persons spiritually stronger since it relates to purity of thoughts and mind. Such purity makes you survive as human being otherwise you are forced to live burdened with sorrow. Similar would be your work worship to make you virtually stronger, in the sense that it will make you survive in your worldly existence. Being spiritual is your inner strength while being virtual is your outer strength. A combine of both these worships would be your overall actual strength.

Before looking to as what is one's religion, we should see what religion is in fact? I have no right to ask any person as to what is your religion? I would have to reply instead as to what is my religion? Religion could by synonymous with righteous way of life. One has to follow the sacred path or right path. What amounts to be sacred? What amounts to be right? Who will say that this path is sacred and rightful? You should follow it on. Do you feel it correct that what others say as sacred or right? You agree to it and you are going to do that. Whether what others say is the only rightful path? Or you have your own capacity to decide about a right step to be followed. This is a scientific fact that the nature has bestowed upon every individual a rationally thinking logical mind. By his own logics an individual can well decide about his rightful path to follow on. There is no need for him to follow as to what others say. Clarity of human logic capacity goes sharper by regular practice, making the individual an all time righteous human being.

See…!!! Any step going to be taken by you, would be either right or wrong one. You understand that and the options are wide open for you to apply your mind carefully. Being a man of reasonable thinking you yourself can decide as to what is right and what is wrong. You can proceed accordingly for the right choice only. I find no reason that somebody should suggest you the right path. You are not supposed to keep sitting idle and wait for somebody to come and make you work upon your project. You should be the master of your own destiny. At the same time where some honest elderly advice is worth considering for a right path, nobody stops you to work upon it. You already know in your conscious mind that you should not do anything wrong for others. By not doing anything wrong to others in itself reciprocates for a right work. You yourself are struggling for your survival in your life then how come you help others? You are not in a position to do so. But if you are not doing anything wrong to others then this is a right path. You are not harming others. You are not hurting others. If possible, you are helping them out as well, within your limited resources. This is a great religion for you and you feel it works.

You are working for yourself. You are working for others. You are working for the society and for betterment of the mankind. That is great. Working sincerely requires concentration and piousness of your mind. Any kind of impurity in mind is going to vitiate your work plan. Same holds good when you are worshipping. Your work would be dependent upon your resourcefulness. May be you are not that resourceful. Never mind. If you are incapable to work for others, but at least you are not harming anybody. Make it a point that this is a great contribution for the betterment of the society. Your work itself is worship and is your religion. A person who worships the God daily but he keeps malicious feelings for others, this is not righteous. May be due to your day to day engagements in your working life you are not able to find time to worship the God. But your work is going to be the worship since you have attained the purity and peace of mind by your pious work. You have achieved the purpose of worship. You are worshipping daily but causing pain to others and hurting them at the same time is of no use. Instead, if you promise with yourself to be extra cautious in not doing anything wrong and to the extent possible helping others in need, itself is a work towards great worship. Your work is big or small that is immaterial. You are dedicating to your work with sincere attitude to perform better. You will experience that it begets peace of mind not only for you but to others as well. Let your religion 'work' on this earth for welfare of the mankind and that would be the great 'worship'.

*"I find no reason that somebody should suggest you the right path. At the same time where some honest elderly advice is worth considering for right path, nobody stops you to work upon it. You already know in your conscious mind that you should not do anything wrong for others. That itself reciprocates for a right work. Your work worship would make you spiritually stronger for your best survival. Make your work to be your worship and that is your pious religion."*

# 2

## NO WORRIES

Human life is full of stress and storms. We are seen worried for one reason or the other in our daily life. Our desires go unending and we fail to make sincere efforts to fulfill them. People are seen blaming as if life is responsible for all their worries. Do we ever think why to blame the life for all worries and stress, we encounter with? Do we think about our contributions in making our life with full of stress? Did we ever support our life by happiness for ourselves? These are the few questions which need honest reply to the point. Life is full of happiness. We need only, is to change our perception towards life. Nature has its own discipline, so is the life. No doubt, when we fail to be disciplined in life, the consequences are to follow. Indiscipline gives rise to stress. Life cannot help, if we do not abide with the disciplinary rules of life.

Where do we go wrong? Is it for that, what we desire we could not get? We tend to forget one thing. We could not get those desires because we did not make required hard work. Then why to worry after all? Make efforts and work hard, your worries would vanish. It is as simple as that. The sole reason of worries in our life is that most of us desire lot many things to get but without making much effort for that. We are so attached to our desires and the moment we find that our desires are not fulfilled, we get into deep worries. We should desist from saying that the life has become hell; rather we have made the life hell by desiring a lot and doing nothing. There is one suggestion. Why to desire for the things at all, if we are not honest in making sincere hard work to get those desires fulfilled? Desires in one's life are endless, so is the endless effort making process for fulfilling such desires. Either stop desiring or desire that only what you honestly think you can achieve that. It is said that desire is the all cause of worries. Yes...!!! It becomes a certain reason of worry when you keep desiring only and do nothing. You desire to become rich. Make efforts or get worries.

People spoil best of their years in keep worrying all the time. They bring worries of their office to home and spoil mind of family members too. We are found worrying for the things which are unseen, not real. We worry because we apprehend that thing to happen. It is lack of our zeal and self-confidence to work upon our worries. You worry due to the fact that you are jobless. You are getting job but no job satisfactions. You worry that you want to leave the job but for want of job security and the obvious apprehension that you may not get any new better job. See...!!! Either you muster the courage to leave your job and struggle to search for a job up to your satisfaction. Or else make up your mind to satisfy yourself in the job you are. Keep worrying is not going to help you out in any manner. It is going to harm you and stress you with serious health issues. Worry is more dangerous than a funeral pyre. Worry burns out the living person while funeral pyre burns the dead.

Let me warn you. Your worry habits are going to adversely affect quality of your life. Your family members too, would be badly affected by it. Worries are quite natural when we face unnatural happenings in our life. Such happenings are not within our control. You have to be mentally strong to overpower such worries, no way. If you are fond of reading good inspirational books then it is the best way to keep away from worries. Love your life and share your worries with your family and the friends you love. You will experience that sharing your worries with people you love, has a soothing effect. You will find that you are relaxed and getting out of your stress. Worry is nothing but is only a state of mind. You can win over it for sure. Never allow the worries to creep in and surround your mind. Be mentally strong. That's it.

*"We need to change our perception towards life. You desire to become rich. Make efforts or get worried. Keep worrying is not going to help you out in any manner. It is going to harm you and stress you with serious health issues. Worry is more dangerous than a funeral pyre. Worry burns out the living person while funeral pyre burns the dead. Love your life and never allow worries to creep in."*

---

# 3

## FOLLOW YOUR INTUITIONS

You would have definitely perceived in your life that you saw something you like, in your dreams, or you think of some person you like. You find that in next few days you get the thing of your liking, what you saw in your dreams. The other morning you met the person who was in your dreams and you so remembered. You were surprised to notice that. It is a false proverb to my understanding that dreams are negative and do not come true. If your thinking is positive and has been imbibed within your inner conscious then make it a point that your dreams could not be negative. Your dreams would come true. Dreams are the images of your sub-conscious mind. What a man thinks the whole day it is settled down in his sub-conscious mind. While the man sleeps his sub-conscious mind works. Now the nature of dreams would be depending upon the qualities of ideas a man is thinking about. Positive dreams are inner signals to keep you moving on right path of your life. You would have to develop such a mental mechanism process that you are able to read those signals and then imbibe them in your life to further work upon.

We need to understand intuition mechanism. Have you ever experienced the power of intuitions in your life or ever analyzed those indicative signals? If you are governing your day to day life according to your intuitive indications then you would be among most successful people of the world. There are people who have suffered number of failures in their life before they could finally succeed. Behind every failure of a man there is hidden message for success provided we are able to stop for a moment and read them out. Successful people could read those intuitive messages and converted it to their advantage. Take for instance; it has happened with you on number of occasions that you remember some beloved person in your mind. Soon after a while your door bell rang up. The moment you opened the door you were surprised to notice that the person you were remembering just now is standing before you. Wonderful...!!! How come? You are amazed to see the person you just remembered. Did you receive intuitive impulses remembering about him? This appears to you nothing less than a miracle. Later you admit that you had the intuition that he was coming. Now another instance, you remembered somebody. The next moment your phone rang up. You received the phone call and to your utter surprise you find that it was the same person on the other side, to whom you just remembered short while ago. This immediately clicks to your mind. Oh...!!! My goodness how it all happened? But it happens, if you take notice of them sensibly.

You would have heard elderly people saying that if your eyelids blink then somebody is remembering you. You happen to receive message from that person soon thereafter. Yes...!!! He admits he was remembering you at that moment. Research studies term this mechanism as 'telepathy' mode to transmit communications from one human mind to the other without using any external aid. Do you believe in numbers? This is known as 'numerology'. You are going for pious work somewhere, in the meantime a motor moves from in front of you. You find that number, on the number plate of the vehicle is same number which you consider to be your lucky number. You noticed that number plate and felt a kind of brightness within your eyes. You find a big stream of hope within your body and mind. You feel flooded with self-confidence. Your mind starts telling that you will be successful in your work, what you are going for. May be you are going for an interview in search of a job. You find to your surprise

8

that you have been declared successful in the said interview. This goes to strengthen your belief in numbers. The motor then crossed with your lucky number was an intuitive message for you.

Such intuitions in your life are not mere ordinary happenings but are some way or the other linked with 'bio-scientific' system of your body. You want to do something but your destiny decides something else, as best suited for you. Your destiny takes you where you are supposed to have been. You would have to make your efforts, the destiny would prepare the best suitable destination for you. You should not take your intuitions lightly. Analyze your intuitions as to why such a thought came to your mind after all? Then connect the dots of your intuitions to the path of your success. If your thoughts are honest then your intuitions would definitely take you on to the success. They will take you on path of achievements and bring you happiness in your life. You just feel and imbibe the indications of your intuitions within yourself and get started in search of it and go well in deep to the 'bio- scientific' reasons of such intuitions. You will get a big wonderful telepathic knowledge out of these intuitions.

*"Your dreams come true provided you have given positive signals to your sub-conscious mind. Behind every failure there remains a hidden message for success provided we are able to decode that. You would have heard elderly people saying that if your eyelids blink then somebody is remembering you. You happen to receive message from that person soon thereafter. Yes...!!! He admits that he was remembering at that moment. Take your intuitions sensibly and work upon them. Intuitions are to help you."*

---

# 4

# FIGHT YOUR FEAR OUT

Fear consciousness is a natural characteristic of human mind. Did you ever think that why a person gets fear in his mind? You will not deny from this fact that fear is a negative state of mind. You have no fear because you have a clean mind. You have fear because you have a guilty mind. You have guilty mind because your intentions are malicious and bad. You have malicious intentions because you think negative. It is person's mind set. Inference of such mind set goes to show that it is an individual who is personally responsible for fear consciousness of his mind. Think positive you will have absolutely no fear.

Why a person gets fear? You might have experienced on number of occasions in your life that whenever you take any step which your mind does not permit but you appear to be helpless at the hands of your heart. You know that what you are going to do is wrong. You should not do it but still you do it. This is negative, making your intention culpable. Fear crops up in the mind of a person when he commits an act which he knows that said act is either legally wrong or morally wrong in the eyes of society. A person being a social animal cannot ignore established social norms in their totality. Only the people who have broken social ties become curse for the society and have no feeling of remorse or fear in their mind. It will we altogether a different subject matter of research that what make people to become hardened towards society and become mentally so insensitive that they have no sense of fear in their mind. This is an abnormal mind set and leads the person towards criminal behavior in the society.

People may argue and have difference of opinion that it is not always the negative thinking which generates fear. A person has a wish and desire to achieve something positive but he is scared whether he will be able to achieve it or not? A person has a life time goal to approach but still he has a fear in his mind till he achieves that goal. Approaching for a goal could never be termed as 'negative thinking' still it generates fear. Is it not contradictory? No…!!! It is not contradictory provided you are working with a determined mind without bothering for results. Once you are worried about results fear would set in your mind naturally. You should have no reason for good results without making needed hard work. Your expectations are wrong without making adequate sincere efforts. Make sure; fear consciousness has to be there. There are motivational stories of great successful people on this earth that despite fears in their pursuits of life, they never surrendered and kept performing. The end result for them has been sure success. So never fear when you are positive.

Oho…!!! Yes. It is agreed and well argued. Buddhist approach is that even having a wish or desire for any achievement amounts to be a negative thinking. Desiring is negative and action is positive. Simply desiring for things, without any action, would generate fear. Desiring for good job in this competitive atmosphere is not bad but making not up to the mark efforts would put you in fear. You have to fight your fear out by your action. If you are approaching your goal with full determination, honesty and confidence, then no force on this earth can stop you from getting success in your life. You would achieve your goals without any trace of fear. People fear death. It is an eternal truth of life that every one of us has to reach death one day. But we are not scared of death and keep performing our action. We need to protect ourselves from fear being generated from 'negative thinking'. Fight your fear out by 'thinking positive'.

*"You have no fear because you have a clean mind. You have fear because have a guilty mind. You have guilty mind because your intentions are malicious and bad. You have malicious intentions because you think negative. Think positive you will absolutely have no fear. Desiring for something without action would generate fear. Fight your fear out by your action."*

# 5

## HAPPY STATE OF MIND

It is very difficult to define happiness. A man is happy in scarcities while the other one remains worried despite all abundance. Happiness is not essentially correlative with material but it is a state of mind. Happiness has different dimensions. This could be depending upon person to person and the situations in which he is living. There could be kind of queries in your mind. A person who is poor, is he happy? A person who is wealthy, he must be happy then? A person who is physically fit with sound health, then he must be happiest one. To be physically sound, one needs sufficient material for healthy food and living conditions. Physical soundness correlates with money. If you have money, there is no need to worry you for healthy food. Physical wellness enhances the happiness perspectives of mind. Material soundness cannot be guaranteed to every person. We are going to have people who are devoid of physical wellness for no money, no food and malnutrition all around. People who are starving, where is the happiness for them? A person full of material resources at his disposal has a lust for earning money by whatever means. He was wasting his health day and night to earn wealth. Now he is wasting his wealth to earn good health. Happiness has no meaning for him despite the fact that he is a rich man. Money may give sense of security but it gives no guarantee for physical wellness of a person.

He is not able to enjoy his choice dish because of food restrictions by the doctor. He is not able to buy happiness for himself because happiness is not a commodity which is sold in markets or in the shopping malls.

There are poor people who are satisfied with whatever money they earn by their honesty and hard labor within limited resources. They are happy to the core of their heart. They get sound sleep in the night and are ready for the next day hard work. Satisfaction is the significant dimension for happy state of mind. Hard workers without lust for money remain satisfied with, what they could earn. Wealthy men, who are burning with lust for money, have restless, sleepless nights. They are able to earn more than their necessities but still they remain mad after money. Lust for money makes one remain unhappy. There is scope for argument that people living below poverty line, need a basic minimum material support from the state so that they are able to sustain physically to work hard. They do not run away from working hard but scarcities make them sick physically as well mentally. States with the help of their welfare policies for poor and weaker sections should buy happiness for their citizen by supporting them. Happiness index initiatives are novel steps in this regard so that sustainable happiness measures could be ensured for all.

The world has witnessed Buddha's material resourcefulness. But very closely he could perceive that desire is the mother of all worries. The worries disturb peace of your mind and there is no reason for you to be happy. He could have very happily enjoyed his princely life but he left home in search of happiness only to become enlightened Buddha. His interactions with worries in the society made him to understand that his princely material was not going to help in his ultimate search for peace and happiness. Mankind's ultimate goal for life is the search for peace of mind. Enlightenment is the state of mind, so is the happiness. Satisfaction has the mental element while dissatisfaction breeds unhappiness. Let us be happy and make others happy too.

*"He was wasting his health day and night to earn wealth. Now he is wasting his wealth to earn good health. Happiness has no meaning for him despite the fact he is a rich man. Search for peace and happiness is the ultimate goal of the mankind. Happiness is the state of mind. It is not sold in the markets or shopping malls. Happiness index initiatives are novel steps in this regard so that sustainable happiness measure could be ensured to all."*

# 6

## YOUR PAST INSPIRES

Live in present, never forget your past and aim for the future. It is an established fact that people get their identity, depending upon their past practices and performances. If past is glorious then chances of future being good are greater but this cannot be said to be a universal rule. A good scientist in the past continues to practice on his extensive research for years with all possibilities to be future Nobel laureate. The past may not be satisfactory but people get inspired from past failures, work more hard and muster their future to be bright. Every person is not born with a silver spoon in his mouth. Those not born with silver spoon have to struggle hard for a better tomorrow. Life is a tale of failures and successes. Sometimes it's more failure than success. Your life failures becoming past make the foundation stone of your future life successes. Nothing succeeds like success. Never forget your past, it inspires.

In India, where socio-economic condition of good number of people is not very satisfactory, they have to struggle for survival in their life since childhood. For such category of poor class of people there is no meaning of, as to what their past was and what would their future be. They are only worried for their present that they could any how arrange the bread for the day to feed their kids. Analytical government data indicate that poverty has increased with passage of time. Now calling for such category of people and advising them to look back to their past it inspires, is very painful. First they should get ideal conditions to survive then only one could expect from them to struggle for a better future.

We come across the instances of world class statesmen like Abraham Lincoln, APJ Abdul Kalam who had to fight acute poverty conditions in their life. They could overcome their hardships since they had firm determination to progress even under adverse circumstances. Even for the people born with silver spoon in their mouth, it is no guarantee that they will continue to have a better future. Despite abundant material resources unless they are vigilant enough to exploit the resources for further development, it is not going to be an easy task for them even.

You are living in present. The chain of events happening in present becomes your past. It is true that you should not be worried about past events. You must be concentrating prospectively forgetting past failures. Adversities in your life would make you strong from within provided you are facing them, without getting depressed. May be your past is full of adversities but it provided you an opportunity to learn from your mistakes and to overcome your adversities by converting them to your advantage. You will only be able to get an advantage out of it provided you are sensitive towards the lessons you had in past under acute worrying conditions.

Never forget your past, may be which was not glorious. Let it be adverse and painful. While suffering through bad times your mind perceives it most. Day by day, this goes on as a matter of past. Your mind keeps working on it and does much mental exercise to defeat adversities. By regular exercise, your mind becomes tough and strong. It is similar to that, your body gets tough and strong by regular physical exercise. Thanks to your past adversities that it conferred you opportunity to develop your mental strength. Past was adverse but your determinations made it happen, towards achievements of your life's goals. Be sensitive, to look back to your past, it inspires.

*"Every person is not born with a silver spoon in his mouth. Those not born with silver spoon have to struggle hard for a better tomorrow. Life is a tale of failures and successes. While suffering through bad times your mind perceives it most and gets stronger. Your life failures becoming past make the foundation stone of your future life successes. Never forget your past, it inspires."*

---

# 7

# LIFE HAS MEANING

Your life has a beautiful meaning for you. You have to live it, up to the objectives that you are born to live. When you would be leaving this world, people will remember that you left behind a tale of meaning, not only to your life but for the people at large. That is the beauty of life. This does not mean that there are no downs in one's life. Rightly says, the proverb that life is full of ups and downs. No doubt, when you are up in your life, it appears to be full of cheers. But the moment when there are downs, we get full of worries. It is quite natural also for us as human beings. The broad day lights have to be followed by dark phases of nights. In the cycle of life we have happy good days followed by sufferings too. Sufferings in human life have more dominating effect over pleasant moments. We cannot be machines. We are psychologically affected by sufferings of life. But this does not mean that we should be down with worries. Keep worrying is not advisable. Worry state of mind is definitely not going to help us out from the downs. We are here to live our life. Accept to your life as it is.

With sun rise the dark phase has to essentially vanish. Living up to the life means developing a strong sense of acceptability with a mindset to keep ready for the downs, at the same time enjoying with the ups in our life. Your life has a meaning for you. Happiness and sufferings are the two sides of the same coin. It is the sufferings of your life which make you realize and enable you to enjoy the phases of happiness in true sense. It is you only who have the potential to make your life meaningful for yourself. Life is not a bed of roses you understand it, so you have to live it. We all have determinations to reach on to our life destinations. We would be able to give meaning to our life if we have decided well considered destinations like peace, happiness brotherhood, human welfare etc.

We take our life journey through different roads. Our ultimate destination would be after all, to be a better human being in search of truth for humanity. All of us would have to pass through these roads with obstacles of various kinds. Some of us may have lesser, while some may have more obstacles. But we never stop our journey of life for the reasons of obstacles. The only best way out is to take life as it is and keep moving on. No other option is available but to keep on negotiating such obstacles by accepting them as this is the way of life.

Negotiate your life because your life has a meaning not only for you and your family but for the people at large as well, in the world around you. You are able to detach yourself as to what is going to happen in your life? You keep on doing what you are supposed to do, be sure you are living your life up to. You are doing well that should be your approach. Goodness begets goodness. If you are good, you are going to get things to be good for you. There is one advice for you. Do not run away from pains. You cannot. Try to feel the pain in your life close to your heart. You will develop a kind of immunity for pains which would strengthen your psycho-somatic system from within, to ever face the sufferings in your life and making your life worth living. Failures in your life never mean that you have no potential to succeed. Do not count your success by your calculations but leave it, up to your life efforts. You just live your life and enjoy it. Life always gives opportunities for everyone for their advancement. If we fail to cash it on at the right moment then who is to be blamed? Think for a moment. Still all is not lost for you. Life still has enough opportunities for you. Make honest efforts and cash it on for your successful future. Always remember your life means. Do not let it go from your hands.

*"Do not run away from pains. You cannot. Try to feel the pain in your life close to your heart. You will develop a kind of immunity for pains which would strengthen your psycho-somatic system from within to ever face the sufferings in your life and making your life worth living. Keep worrying is not advisable. Life has enough opportunities for you."*

---

# 8

# THE GREAT PEOPLE

We always need inspiration from great people to progress in our life. People, who are great, are the people who have genuine concern for everyone irrespective of any consideration. They have no consideration whether to which community you belong to, especially when the society has become more sensitive based upon caste and religion. Great people are not born, great people are made. They become great while living and working in this society itself. How would they become an inspiration for you? Because looking to their life history, struggle and achievements you feel within yourself, to be much on their lines, you are also progressing. They become an ideal for you. Why to name any great personality to describe on? Their greatness itself must be considered as a trait to be followed up. You start feeling determined that you also want to be great. Your greatness lies in the fact that you want to be a better human being. Achievements in your career opportunities are very significant. Never think like this that people are very rare who become successful in their career opportunities. But yes…!!! People are very rare who were successful in their career, at the same time they were also great people of their times.

Meaning thereby, the greatness is much more extra than merely being successful in your career. One day you become successful in your career but still, you are not satisfied with yourself since you wanted to be great. Along with your journey through your career, you always kept making efforts to move on the path, which would take you to the greatness. Great people are nothing different than we the ordinary people. They are as simple as you are. They are as generous as you are. But what makes them different that remains a curiosity for us? The difference is quite apparent which is visible at the very first instance. Do we have the vision, to perceive that? Watch carefully, you have the vision to perceive that. Always keep it in your mind that merely perception would not be sufficient. Practicing on it is more important a fact than a simple perception. There are people who pretend to be honest but the people who are great, they are honest truly but they never pretend to be honest. They are honest body impersonate. That is the difference. This honesty reflects in their personality. They live with honesty, till the last day of their life. They think for welfare of the people. They love to work for human welfare and dedicate their life for the sake of the mankind. They never expect any certificate from this world, regards they are honest. It is their inner self-conscience which gives them the needed strength so to protect on their perception and practice. They would live honest and they would die honest. They always pray to the Almighty that even in their distant dreams they should not act in a manner which is in any manner prejudicial to human beings. It is not that simple which so appears to be. Honesty is the single tenet of one's life which centrally controls and regulates the daily actions of a man. You may be successful but you are not honest then success is of no meaning to you. You may keep pretending to be honest while you live but make sure you are not going to die honest. Greatness prevails around when you die honest, this the entire world knows. Greatness was established without much publicity provided you died honest. That's it. Be great.

*"Watch carefully, you have the vision to perceive that. Always keep it in your mind that merely perception would not be sufficient. Practicing on is more important a fact than a simple perception.*

*Great people are nothing different than we the ordinary people. There are people who pretend to be honest but the people who are great, they are honest truly but they never pretend to be honest. They are honest body impersonate. That is the difference. They would live honest and they would die honest."*

---

# 9

# SUFFERING HUMANITY

Are we concerned about the people who are starving? Do we feel about the children who are suffering from malnutrition? Do we worry about them who are dying of hunger? We expect from them that they should work. They do not work that is why they suffer. They want to get something without doing anything. If they are dying from hunger then they are to be blamed for that. Well, they should work. Who stops them from working and earning their livelihood? Putting in hard work needs physical wellness. Because of their starving conditions, they feel sick and weak. Are they physically sound to work for? People may say that it is none of their business. But let the governments to generate resources and engage them in work. Did the caretakers of the government system worry about the migrant poor labor, who were locked down following hasty and defective decision makings, in the wake of novel corona virus Covid-19 outbreak? With small kids in their laps and belongings on their head, they were made to walk down thousand miles on foot via roads and railway tracks without food and shelter. Humanity suffered that the innocent labor communities were killed on roads and railway tracks. It is for democratically elected welfare governments to ensure measures for such people at least for the sake of humanity. In such kind of human tragedies the governments are supposed to be much sensitive to human welfare and do not play political blunders. But the governments did not visualize such scenario, failing on all the fronts and making it the worst human suffering of the century.

What would happen when the governments go careless and leave them to starve and die? Where goes then, the concept of welfare governance? It is welfare of whom? It is welfare by whom? One should reasonably expect from the caretakers of the governments that they should be welfare oriented. But what to do if they are not much worried about their people who are suffering with acute scarcities? Most of the countries across the globe have democratic patterns of governance. They are 'of the people' and they are 'by the people'. But when it actually comes to governance, they apparently look that they are not 'for the people'. Worst condition is of those countries which are full of corruption in public governance. The so called public leaders, in connivance with officers of the state, bungle out with public money which is meant for public welfare measures. We are witness to the fate of various government schemes relating to public health and poverty alleviation programs. Cases of criminal misappropriation of public funds have been reported in large scales, by crushing aside the humanitarian interests of poor and weaker sections, while the legal administration appears to be helpless to get the things in order. When the leadership itself has gone corrupt so deep then it becomes very difficult to control the lower cadres and one looks on hopelessly for no way out.

Welfare measures are for those members of public who are poor and belong to the weaker sections of the society. It is just to support them and their kids, so that they can survive and progress. They have no option but either to live without resources or to die empty stomach. The same is the condition for their children who are suffering from malnutrition, diseases, living in unhygienic conditions. Families have no money to get nutritious food for them or get them medicines either. Children die for want of proper medical care because public health measures are eaten away by corruption. Even if they get cure they are not going to have healthy nutrition. Getting weak and weak, one day they would leave away this world. They never came in this world to live. They came, struggled for their survival but they could not survive. Nobody did come out to help them and support them. Even if those children who survive, could not get proper schooling for the same reasons of acute crisis in the management of government run schools. Child labor full with exploitation is very common, since with no education they had to go for work and survive, sacrificing their childhood dreams.

People may rightly argue that it was the government's job. Why the governments failing in all that for saving the life of weaker needy people? Do the governments go deliberate after they grab power by petty politics? People are not in a condition to know that the governments were gone careless. How could they know? It needs for them to be mentally alert. They are with empty stomach, sick and suffering from all weakness. Please, do not expect them to be mentally alert. This is the kind of situation the public officials are taking advantage of, because the people who are weak are not in a position to speak. They know that such weak, empty stomach and badly exhausted people are no potential threat to their power politics. They are not in a position to oppose them and demand for their welfare rights. Humanity demands, a system free of any political corruption and its share of resources so that it survives on this earth with human dignity.

*"Most of the countries across the globe have democratic patterns of governance. They are 'of the people' and they are 'by the people'. But when it actually comes to governance, they apparently look that they are not 'for the people'. Humanity demands welfare measures for those who are poor and weaker sections of society. Welfare governments should not run away from their duty to serve their people."*

# 10

## GO FOR ACTION

Your life plan has a law of action to be followed. You will plan, you will act upon and you will achieve. Planning merely would not be sufficient unless acted upon with an intention to get the plan executed. It would be a very difficult question as how your action should be carried on? But this difficulty will be eased out, once you are coming out with full determination to work upon your plan. Your action should be an act of yours which would take you on a rightful path in your life. What would be the rightful path for you? Thinking for your own self, being self centric or having broad approach to think for other as well. Helping others is great but merely thinking would not do. Philanthropic is a person next to God, in the materialistic world of today. What should one do then? He should perform actions keeping in his mind the objectives for his life first. He would have to then manage for the resources also, to get those objectives fulfilled. For managing resources he has to perform action regularly.

Law of action emphasizes to keep performing sincerely and honestly without an expectation of fruits of action. It is quite natural that the feeling for fruits of action comes in our mind. The fruits of hard work are always sweet. A person has to start his action to get the fruits of success. He should know that he is not going to get fruits without action. Whether he would succeed or he would fail?

Everybody wants to succeed following his action. The person should, because that's only is the positive approach. Possibilities of success would be on much higher side because your well planned action is going to side track chances of failures. A person targets his future and prepares a line of action, so as to get through it. You cannot have a plan without a specific goal. Any line of action is going to flop which is without aims and object. Or else, it would be an endless journey in futility. Therefore, first fix your target that what you want to achieve in your life. A man with a well defined goal, would successfully be in a position to make his well defined plans. This will ensure execution plan accurate and time bound. Law of action also presupposes that life journey should have a destination so that one keeps acting upon to reach up to that.

For younger generations who are struggling hard in search of their future career, philosophy of action is very practical and needs to be inculcated in their life style. There are young who have enough resources to struggle, on the other hand are those with poor resources. It is noticed that they are more interested in short cuts rather than working hard. This should be always remembered that there is no short cut of success. They have to concentrate only to pursue their action. The roadmap of success has to be completed in its entirety and not through short cuts. It should be agreed that with the help of needed resources standard of action would be on much higher levels. It is noticed that our youngsters wish to perform their actions sincerely but for the resources and poor infrastructure they withdraw in between, or compromise with what they get. In search for better infrastructure and to satisfy their appetite of performances they move overseas. Instead of providing them better infrastructure system blames them to be responsible for brain drain. This is absolutely unfair. Let the system provide them with basic infrastructure, they are ready to plan and act for the nation and get success. The law of action would prove to be more practical and beneficial when system provides for equality of opportunities and availability of resources to all, so that they can concentrate much to their actions and utilize their talent most beautifully.

*"Law of action emphasizes to keep performing sincerely and honestly without an expectation of fruits of action. It is quite natural that the kind of feeling for fruits of our action comes in mind. Law of action also presupposes that life journey should have a destination so that one keeps acting upon to reach up to that. Possibilities of success would be on much higher side subject to execution of well planned action."*

---

# 11

# WISDOM OF GREAT THINKERS

Great people are those who do not live for themselves but they live for others. Great thinkers do not think for themselves but they think for welfare of the mankind. What makes a person to be a great thinker? A man, who has a well-developed mind, is the centre of thinking process. Animals too, have the capacity to think and express that even. Biology of human mind makes them to think much well, faster and in a much logical manner. Notice the behavior of an animal. Hit that animal by any stick or stone. The animal does not either bite the stick or the stone. It attempts to bite the man who uses that stick or the stone. That is the kind of understanding the animal has. We human beings with a bigger mind are supposed to be better thinkers and for a better purpose.

Execution of thoughts is a unique feature in social systems. Apart from being strictly individual, it is extended further as community thinking patterns, benefitting human existence on this earth. You think big or think small. You think good or think bad. It all depends upon you. Engage power of your mind by means of rigorous and continuous thinking process mixed with genuine societal concerns, you will find that not only it comes out stronger but proves to be much refined too. Studies reveal that on an average people use only twenty five percent capacity of their mind, therefore an expected performance from a human mind goes average or even below. Those who use their mind on a percentage with much higher levels they get most expected and best results. Thus practice your mind with a bigger percentage of its use and see the miracle. Thinkers do not have any bigger mind than average mind but they think differently to handle problematic social situations.

Great thinkers are no special people. They also are just like us. They also have a similar thinking mind but they think differently. They all the time keep practicing their mind with constructive and welfare oriented thoughts with genuine concern for the people who are deprived. They are able to think big because they are not narrowing minded and never self centered. Why the wisdom of such thinkers make them great? They dare to think into prevailing customary social evils. The painful social discriminatory practices based upon religion, race, caste, origin are divisive but are recognized even in modern educated civilizations. Such thinkers come out with suggestive measures so as, peace and wellness prevails in the society. They are made of such a metallic mind that they do not remain a silent spectator over wrong things happening in society, while they had a choice to remain silent as least concerned. They will use their mind for social remedies to the social problems. The administrators of the social system are expected to implement the wisdom of social thinkers through their socio-economic policy making so as to attain best possible results in the welfare and well being of the mankind on this earth.

Their worry of political thinkers is for political administration to be good for general welfare of the people. It is politicians who claim to be everything fair in love, war and politics but the wisdom of great political thinkers cries out when they witness modern politicians busy in high jacking the entire system by indulging in all corrupt means and jeopardizing the social and economic interests of innocent people. Great thinkers are for just, reasonable and fair without discrimination of any kind. Do we think that we are up to it? We have failed in view of prevalent injustices social, economic and political.

*"Engage power of your mind by means of rigorous and continuous thinking process mixed with genuine societal concerns, you will find that not only it comes out stronger but proves to be much refined too. Studies reveal that on an average people use only twenty five percent capacity of their mind, therefore an expected performance from a human mind goes average or even below. Those who use their mind on a percentage with much higher levels, they get most expected and best results."*

---

# 12

## YOUR PEACEFUL MIND

You search for peaceful minds around you. It is found that much small numbers of such minds are there in present competitive world. There is hectic rush on the roads to beat one another. You will find that people are getting disturbed for one reason or the other in their daily race for bare survival. Some do not have peace of mind because of lost opportunities while others are disturbed since they could not avail opportunities. The reason is quite apparent as better opportunities are lesser while claimant numbers keeps rising high. But never mind, if you want to be on top of the world, it will always keep disturbing your mind. Disturbing in the sense not negative but it is a positive state of your mind. It does not mean that you get discouraged and lose your heart. You have accepted the challenge to be on top of the world, so you are working on your target. Let the people around you say that you are looking disturbed. In fact you are not disturbed but you are concentrating and content within yourself. Your mind has reached to a level that now it is not a disturbed mind but it has become a searching mind on way to its destination. People would not be able to understand your mindset and would unnecessarily talk unusual. A searching mind always works much harder and is never disturbed till some external factor disturbs its concentration against your will. Remember that a concentrated searching mind is a peaceful mind and you do not permit anyone to enter to your mind. If you want to achieve best from life then during watchful moments of your mind, you must be sensitive by living in present and keep focusing the set targets.

Are you able to focus your mind to the point you wish to? May be there are situations that despite your sincere efforts you find that you are not getting your mind focused. Have you ever thought as to why you are not in a position to focus your mind? When you are working upon one idea but at a time you also encounter with other thoughts in your mind which are out of relevance at the moment then it is going to be quite obvious that you lose focus of your mind at one point. If you fail to have a focused mind, then by the end of the day, you will find that you achieved nothing despite all out efforts made by you all the time. Your efforts go waste and that is enough to get your peace of mind out. You lost to complete the set target for the day, so also you lost peace of mind as well. Obviously thoughts keep coming to your mind by nature. But while you are concentrating on a particular thought, you would have to take all precautions to ensure that others thoughts which are not related to the idea you are working upon do not come to your mind. If you are not able to stop them you are not able to focus your mind. So whatever you work for the whole day, you do not get expected result. Look for the reasons behind, you would find that you did not start the day with a focused mind. All went wrong throughout the day and you got disturbed. Focused mind means when entire concentration of your mind has been pointed to the target like function of a convex lens. This lens concentrates the sun energy on a single point and makes the object burn. When you start aiming at the target you see nothing around except the single point of your target. This is the 'focused mind' and the rest is the history. Focused mind always accelerates your working potential and enhances capacity building process of your body and mind. In focused searching mind settles the peaceful mind.

*"A searching mind always works much harder and is never disturbed till some external factor disturbs its concentration against your will. If you want to achieve the best from life then during watchful moments of your mind you must be sensitive by living in present and keep focusing the set targets. You want to be on the top then make sure disturbances would keep coming. To avoid disturbances, practice to focus your mind. Focused mind always accelerates your working potential and enhances capacity building process of your body and mind. In focused searching mind settles the peaceful mind."*

# 13

## THE TRYING MOMENTS

Life is a very beautiful journey for those who have resources to enjoy it. But not all people have resources. They live in scarcities and life is not that beautiful for them. But still they have to survive somehow. There are very tough times for them to keep fighting through entire life. We have majority of such families all across the globe which suffer through trying times, all the time. This is not good for any civilization but it could be witnessed anytime. Being a sensitive man you are not in a position to overlook that. You feel the kind of restlessness within, if you were capable to do something for them. Present world is in an urgent need of such helping hands that should come out and take the reins of such systems into their own hands. This would happen and time would see to it. Come on…!!! Friends.

As a young man you make a target for your life to be achieved. First essential achievement must be your future career. You find that you do not have all that needed resources easily available to you so that you could struggle on. Your parents keep supporting you by putting themselves under various hardships. You also understand that your parents also have their own limitations to fulfill with other family obligations. You start feeling that why your parents should be get burdened for fulfilling your requirements. This is what you are put in trying times when you are struggling hard for your career at the same time you are also coping up with your financial adversities so that you can sustain during such times. It is no doubt tough but it makes you strong from within.

Never have any complain with your life that why adversities are for you? This feeling will discourage you and weaken you from inside. Take your life the way it is. Love it that you got an opportunity to make your life beautiful the way you wish. Keep it in your mind that you were not born with a silver spoon in your mouth. Always pray the Almighty that He should put you with any number of challenges and problematic situations but at the same time He should give you the strength to face those problems. Why to worry about testing times? Natural rule is that there is no problem without solutions. You are not supposed to run away from your problems. You have no choice either. This feeling would give you a rare kind of strength and would inspire you to fight your trying times. Never be disheartened. Life decides to put individuals in trying times so that they develop immunity against adversities. You are man with strong characters and firm determination since adversities in your life gave you the opportunity to train your mind to act through trying times.

You should take it in positive sense that the nature has selected you for testing times and train you properly. Because the nature has observed in you the kind of metal, that can sustain the adversities and emerge as a winner to work not only for your daily pursuits but also in the interest of the mankind on this earth. The inference must be that you should never be scared of trying times. Even if you are scared of it, which is quite natural, you should prepare yourself psychologically to deal with it. Your trying times could be long drawn and on occasions you will find hard pressed, feeling as if you are going to be defeated. May be you are going to lose even. Never mind. You are made for such rigorous trials only to be the winner at last. You will be amazed to hear to your inner voice, keep reminding you that you are made strong enough. Life is like this only. Your trial would go on to ensure you that you are the ultimate winner, for all that you intended to achieve for yourself and for your fellow human beings.

*"Never have any complain with your life that why adversities are for you? This feeling will discourage you and weaken you from inside. Take your life the way it is. Love it that you got an opportunity to make your life beautiful the way you wish. Keep it in your mind that you were not born with a silver spoon in your mouth."*

———————————————————————

# 14

## FOR THE MANKIND

We as human beings are made for each other. We are beautiful creations of this nature. We are watching that beauty of the environment, the flora and the fauna, the rivers and the mountains, is going down with passage of time. Where all that beauty of nature has gone? There is marked degradation in human conduct too. We as a creation of nature wish to love and be loved. We as a human being are for the human beings. We are supposed to support them and not to suppress them, as being fellow human beings. You always feel sad to concede this bitter truth that people around you are put to lot many sufferings due to worldly manipulations. There are rulers and the ruled ones. The rulers consider them to be superior ones and on whom they establish their rules are considered by them to be inferior ones. There are people who are privileged, at the same time a large number of people are put in under privileged category. Why this inequality persists? It is in the nature of socio-economic inequality. It cannot be by nature. It is manmade inequality which has been made to persist, everyone knows it. But who cares? History reveals that the rulers have a mindset which has no feeling for humanitarian values. Rare were the great rulers who had respect for the mankind and they worked for their welfare. History today remembers them for their contribution in the betterment of the mankind. Opposite to that, history is full with the tales of such rulers who were cruel and unkind. Their dictatorship tendencies by no standard could benefit the mankind. Individually they could gain to satisfy their fanatic lust for power which was absolutely unnatural. The rule of nature that every person is born equal though sounds good but has been flouted in each and every era. That is the tragedy of the mankind on this earth.

When a child is born on this earth he does not know as which religion he belongs to? Or to which caste he belongs to? By the time the child develops maturity of understanding we make him aware about the particular religion or caste he belongs. Before that he is absolutely innocent about his surroundings. He mixes up with children of his age group, plays with them and shares mutual feelings as true fellow human beings. We start polluting his innocent pure mind. We tell him that his religion or caste is different from others. We talk about the distinction as to high caste and low caste. That he should keep at a distance from children of other castes and religions. We put in his mind the seeds of difference which is converted into mutual hatred ultimately. With the passage of time the same innocent child becomes a totally different man. Now he starts identifying himself as a particular caste or faith. He starts maintaining distance with people from different religion, caste, and region and with different language. We should not forget that in long run bitter feeling of such caste and religious differences among communities lead to violent happenings even to the extent of bloodshed.

Please do not blame our youth for all that. This could have been well prevented for a better world if we had groomed them to respect human feelings. All the blame is with us. We failed in taking all proper care in educating our children that they are for the mankind on this earth. Every religion advocates for humanity. We forgot to inculcate in their mind that all religions on this earth speak for fraternity and mutual brotherhood. We should remember that no religion on this earth would be safe if the humanity is put at risk. Protecting mankind is our collective responsibility.

*"There is a marked degradation in human conduct. We as a human being are for the human beings. We are to support them and not to suppress. We are to be blamed in spoiling innocent minds of our children who develop mutual hatred among communities with the passage of time. Every religion advocates for humanity. We should remember that no religion on this earth would be safe if the humanity is put at risk. Protecting mankind is our collective responsibility."*

---

# 15

## VISION FOR SOCIETY

May I put some questions to you? Kindly allow me. You would be surprised as to what the kind of my questions would be? Nothing like that please. No surprise...!!! There are very simple questions for you. As what is the vision of your life? What the kind of dreams you possess in your mind? What you wish to achieve for and gift to your life? When do you propose to fulfill your dreams? May be you have fulfilled already? Are you sure? Or else, if yet to be fulfilled? Why...!!! How long you will take to get it on? What did you say? No visions...!!! As yet.

The questions must be very usual and much on expected lines. I am putting up these questions to you with a great deal of hope in my mind. If I am not wrong, kindly allow me to say that we all of us, on this earth, are born with certain purpose. We all possess unique talent and a mindset to be visionary for the world and to live up to that. We always look for a life which could be proved to be meaningful. Such meaning to our life would allow us to die in peace. When we leave this world with an imprint back that would justify our inner soul to the core that Yes...!!! You had a vision. You pursued that and left behind an impact back to the world, before you left us sad and weeping.

What the kind of your vision could be? Your future career would be one of the immediate visions of your life. Unless you have a safe and satisfied future, it is going to affect your pursuits to get your visions adverse. You should think for a good small family to live with happily. Without having a good career to earn with sufficiently, it would not be possible for you to further dream big. Your parents are an integral part of your small family. You cannot afford to ignore your parents. Once you did that, whether knowingly or unknowingly, it is going to damage you and your future visions. There are recent trends seen in modern times, people leaving their parents behind in old age homes. That is not any visionary approach. When your parents are not happy, how come you are going to be happy? Make it a point then you will not be able to pursue your visions.

You must have a vision to work for a society in which you are living. Do you feel that all is going on well in your society? You are not ready to agree with it by your heart. You feel that your society is not happy. People in society do suffer with miseries like poverty, physical weakness, health related problems, schooling of their kids, malnutrition and the kind. Are you in a position to help them? You want to help them but you don't have enough financial resources to do so. This becomes the cause of worry for you. You are a man with a vision not merely limited to your own family interest but you also think for the good of the people at large. Simply keeping on thinking is not going to help you out. You need to come forward and work for it without compromising your family interest. Your family members would be your real strength behind to support you while you are out to pursue your visions. A society which lacks happiness cannot give you a happy nation. Happiness of a few who are socially and economically capable cannot be the reason for others prosperity. It could not be any happiness index of the nation either. You have vision about the happiness of your nation with extended global happiness dimensions. You would be able to achieve that, once you see that your society is getting happier. Keep making people happy and work pursuing that.

*"We all possess unique talent and a mindset to be visionary for the world and to live up to that. We always look for a life which could be proved to be meaningful. Such meaning to our life would allow us to die with peace. You pursued your vision for a happy and prosperous society and left behind an impact back to the world, before you left us sad and weeping. Simply keeping on thinking is not going to help you out. A society which lacks happiness cannot give you a happy nation."*

---

# 16

## VALUE YOUR CHARACTER

Human behavior is a gift of nature irrespective of gender distinction between a male or female. They are beautiful creations on this earth, made for each other to love and to be loved. An expression of love between them is by nature. It would be against the nature if a man is not attracted towards a woman or a woman is not attracted towards a man. They are moved by feelings of nature being a man or woman. Such attraction is not merely physical but it is more of emotional. One must be curious to know about those circumstances which could be significant to define the conduct of a person. The purity of human relationships is spoiled by individual characters in such relationships.

There could be certain compelling circumstances created by the society itself. Where man is in need of money, the other man intends to financially help him. That would be immoral if he is subjected to exploitation, by the man who helped him. But it happens. People do exploit to the extent you cannot imagine. You cannot limit expectations of the people, whether good or bad. You cannot stop persons to measure one's expectations from the parameters of morality? This could be individual perception of a person. Others would also be governed by the same perception without having any understanding of their own. This only is the social trend to measure character of individuals in the society.

Mostly such perceptions are seen to be unilateral which could not be justified in given circumstances.

It could be easily seen that society links individuals with their sexual character. This character varies from one civilization to the other. In one society it could be blameworthy whereas the other society may have its own justifications. Mutual attraction between a man and woman could be quite emotional. Their love and affection is natural and pure to the core of their heart. That has nothing to do with any sexual or physical relationship. But the social perceptions could have its own suspicions, without any basis, which need not to be answered. That should be the strength of your character. You are maintaining the purity of human relationships and you are clean by your thoughts. That's it, since you are answerable to yourself.

Who will certify your character? You might have seen authorities very confidently issuing character certificates to individuals. Isn't it looking to be ridiculous? What they do know about the character of an individual? And how come? But you cannot help. That's the system you have to go with it. Always keep in your mind that you are the master of your character. Your conscious heart gives you the certificate the kind of character you are. You do not need any certificate from the people who are nose deep full with immorality. You are committed to help a person who is in need of it, that is your character. You are honest by your heart and mind. You never allow any foul idea against any individual to enter in your mind. When you watch injustice being done to the people of weaker and underprivileged sections of the society, your heart comes out crying and you are not a silent spectator. You decide to fight for it and raise voice against the corrupt system. That is your character. You never mind what others say. Your mind is full with compassion. Your heart is always just and fair. You know, you bear a strong moral character. Never bother for a certificate from anyone.

*"Always keep in your mind that you are the master of your character. Your conscious heart gives you the certificate the kind*

*of character you are. You do not need any certificate from the people who are nose deep full with immorality. You are committed to help a person who is in need of it, that is your character. You are maintaining the purity of human relationships and you are clean by your thoughts. You are honest by your heart and mind."*

---

# 17

# OLD HABITS DIE HARD

A man becomes slave to his habits. Slavery is good or not that is totally a different issue. But being slave to good habits would definitely be appreciated. There are good habits and bad habits too. Now it depends upon you whether you are picking up good habits or bad one. Developing kind of habits is also directly proportional to the kind of company of people you are living in. Definitely associating with people who are practicing good habits is going to benefit you. Living with people of bad company is going to harm you. You are supposed to be a keen observer. It is not necessary that all the time you are getting company of good people. May be such people do not let you to be in their company. In that event you will be a distant observer while learning their good habits. You have to be full of cautions while developing your habits. Your habits are going to determine your future life. Old habits die hard. That is a perfect saying. Your bad habits are potent enough in not only spoiling you but they would affect those people as well who are close to you.

Getting up early in the morning is good habit. Going to bed early in the night and to rise up early in the morning, should be your daily habit irrespective of the season whether it is winter or summer. You have a lot of work to do as you have planned for the whole day. Getting up early after a sound sleep, gives you an added psychological advantage in planning your routine for the day carefully in a very peaceful morning environment. Think of developing your writing habit. Writing skills being an art apart, it is a creation of your thinking mind. This habit is going to be a psychological asset for you in your life. It is not only going to make you strong from inside but would also inculcate in you the kind of confidence in your personality, which is unparallel. You would feel this development personally provided you make an early beginning. Try to experience it on your own.

You are told a number of times by your parents that you should make it a habit, to get up early in the morning by 5 am. Also that you should go to your bed in the night between 9 pm to 10 pm. There are studies revealing that human mind needs 7 hours to 8 hours of good sleep, for its best performance next morning. Start doing that from today itself. You would find that it is going to be a very tough battle for you. For two or three days in the beginning, you would somehow manage to get up around 5 am, but it becomes very difficult for you to continue it further. You soon, go back to your old habits. You continue to try this again and again. You find that it is not easy, to win over your old habits. Give them a tough fight with a determined mind. Make sure that you are going to win this battle by means of a concerted effort within a month's time. However, according to functioning patterns of human mind, 21 days time would be enough for its conditioning to pick up the new habit. Be sure that you must make it a regular effort. Now you will develop a habit of an early riser. You will now get the opportunity, to be in touch with freshness of the nature in the morning hours. The heavenly pleasure you are going to enjoy, in these early hours of the day, you would have no words to explain. You would just feel it within yourself and strengthen you. The kind of energy you have gained during these peaceful early hours of the day would make you successful in any stage of your life. Develop this sole good habit of being an early riser you will see the difference that other bad habits automatically would not find any place in your mind. You will have a plan for the day which will keep you engaged constructively for the whole day leaving no time for negative thoughts. Be a slave of good habits. Do it, you will feel it.

*"Developing kind of habits is also directly proportional to the kind of company of people you are living in. Definitely associating with people who are practicing good habits is going to benefit you. Living with company of bad people is going to harm you. Develop the habit of an early riser and plan your whole in the freshness of the morning."*

---

# 18

## HEALTHY SOUL

There are philosophic opinions about the soul whether it actually exists? Communities of certain faiths believe in rebirth of human beings and their past birth. Belief is that human body dies while the soul never dies and it is immortal. There are pleas about departure of soul from one human body and its union with a new human body. There is no scientific evidence to show life after death, on this earth in the form of rebirth. The moment a human body dies it is destroyed. It starts decomposing immediately after, like any other animal or living organism. My simple explanation about soul relates with the 'self' of a human being. His own 'self' or her own 'self'. The kind of human values and perceptions a person has, within his or her own 'self'. The values he consciously possesses and has the active knowledge about his possessions. His knowledge about own self that he has taken birth as human being, so he has to prove his worth by his good deeds. Not only his knowledge about himself but about other human beings too, so that he was able to do something for them when it is so required. When a person is dead his existence is no more on this earth. He and his values only would be remembered after he departs from this world. He was a man of highest values and a great soul who lived on this earth. You have to live only once on this earth. There are no second innings of human life. Let the man rest in peace while he is live by his good deeds. Let then his soul rest in peace. Definitely his 'self' will go to rest in peace after the man is dead. If you are man of values you will be remembered as great soul, otherwise not.

A healthy body has a healthy mind. It could be other way round too. How come without a healthy mind one could expect to be a healthy body? Human mind plays a very significant role in keeping human body healthy and so the healthy 'self'. Your healthy 'self' depends upon positivity of your thoughts. This only is going to prevail in the form of your pious soul. Feel about the kind of 'self' while you live. What happens after death when your dead body is destroyed after cremation? Those who performed your last rites they witnessed that you were burnt to ashes on the cremation ground. You were buried deep inside the ground then your body was decomposed leaving skeleton behind. It was difficult to identify that it were you only. There was no occasion for you to feel your 'self' after you die. Try to feel your 'self' while you live. This feeling could only be possible when your own 'self' is full with purity of actions and reactions. You have to perform actions. Your positive actions would result into positive reactions while negative ones are bound to yield negativity only. You feel just when your values go negative, your actions also go negative and accordingly your 'self' is also going to be. That's my simple explanation in favor of a 'healthy soul'. It is nothing but the living values of your living mind, in a living body. When you live, your values live and your 'self' lives, making thereby a 'healthy soul' after you depart from this world. The man with values then becomes a departed soul when he dies. The 'soul' would be devoid of any 'health' if your own 'self' lacked purity of thoughts and values while you were living. Make a healthy soul which the death could never destroy. It is only possible by your human like deeds. You never thought of harming others. You did to the best of your capacities to help others feeling to be complete in your 'self'. You are now immortal born to live forever.

*"My simple explanation about soul relates with the 'self' of the human being. What happens after death when your dead body is destroyed? Those who performed your last rites they witnessed that you were burnt to ashes. You were buried deep inside the ground then your body was decomposed leaving skeleton behind. Make a healthy soul which the death could never destroy. Let the man rest in peace while is live by his good deeds. Let then his soul rest in peace. You are now immortal born to live."*

# 19

## NEED SELF IMPROVEMENT

Today you are living in a competitive world, so putting in your struggles to beat the competition. Whether it is your academic career or it is your efforts in search for a suitable employment or any professional pursuit, on every stage you have to go through big competitions. You are a businessman and dealing in production of consumer goods. There are several other manufacturing companies in the market which are making similar products with minor improvements and proving them to be good success. Life is not static it stands for an unending journey for an unknown destination, where you feel yourself to renounce this world. Improvement literally means to do something for further betterment over existing levels whether talking in terms of business gains or self improvement. It is a continuous process which you have to keep pursuing without any break. It is in fact your personal decision to reach on a particular level of improvement. It could be exclusively for your personal achievements or for the sake of society at large.

The people in the society must be looking at you with a desperate hope. They trust you in the sense that you are capable to perform. You have to keep ready yourself for them too because they are looking at you with very optimistic eyes. On your way to perform there could be lot many obstacles you will come across but you would have to face them by means of your sustained self improvement. Some of the obstacles could be part and parcel of your initiatives but many of them are engineered by your opponents. You might have noticed it very closely while you make efforts for improvement a good number of people, pretending to be your well wishers, start pulling your legs. They see your improvement with a jealous eye. They will go to the extent to harm you from behind the curtain. You are so innocent and positive that you do not doubt their intentions. You have no reason to distrust them since you consider them to be your well wishers. You allow them to come close to you but you are mistaken. They are able to damage self improvement initiatives you are making. You need to be extra careful particularly under the circumstances where you fear of any kind of harm from such people.

You need self improvement because you do not believe in status quo. Improvement instinct is by nature and is inbuilt in human personality, so you are. With a winner's attitude you continue in effort making for your life targets. You are an achiever of different kind forgetting one achievement and aiming for others. You are of a kind of metal that you are not satisfied with what you achieve for yourself but you are more satisfied with what you achieve for others. People may not be up to the level to understand the objectives of your life. You have no need to explain them all that. People may even on occasions hint at you that you are gone insane. It would only be the level of your regular self-improvement which is going to shield you from such negative remarks of the people around you. Believe in yourself all the time. Consider for a while what others say but act upon only what your mind suggests. Criticisms are good particularly by those who come out with positive mindset. There are people who criticize you with a malicious and negative orientation to discourage you. Take on criticisms with a sportsman spirit of self improvement and forget about the rest. Your mind would never go wrong. Even if it happens to be wrong due to errors of facts it is subject to rectification.

*"Life is not static it stands for an unknown journey for an unknown destination, when you feel yourself to renounce this*

*world. You might have noticed it very closely that while you make efforts for your improvement good number of people pretending to be well wishers start pulling your legs and see your improvement with a jealous eye. Criticisms are good for self improvement particularly by those who come out with positive mindset and they are worth concerned for your betterment."*

---

# 20

## DEVELOP WRITING HABITS

Try to develop writing habits because it is best method to attain concentration of mind. Without a concentrated mind you will not be able to come out with ideas. Writing habits could not be developed over night. It is a gradual process which could prolong for years altogether. Human mind is full of numerous ideas, good or bad. For a healthy society insistence should be that good ideas must prevail so that a constructive environment is made all around. The ideas which come into human mind, when are converted into writing then other people are also benefited by those ideas. The ideas play a very significant role in policy making and development of any nation. The world civilization has been witness to this very fact that the writings of great writers have proved to be big saviors to the interests of the mankind on this earth.

I have put up above in my note that writing habit is a good device for a person to attain concentration of his mind. A large number of good literatures emphasize for concentration of human mind as an important tool for creativity and production. Thinking is considered to be the best exercise of human mind particularly when your mind is thinking mathematically. For being a good writer you are also supposed to be a good reader of prolific literature of your times. It helps in generating much fruitful thoughts due to confluence of ideas of other best authors of all the times. A regular exercise of mind or of body gives mental strength to the mind and physical strength to the human body respectively. When you start developing into writing habits and convert your thoughts into writing then you become much more careful about your mental exercise for the reasons that now your writings would be presented into published form. Your writings should come into public domain so that people are benefitted by your novel ideas. You should now be cautious about public response to your writings. Kindly welcome criticisms of your conscious readers, when it is accepted positively it triggers further improvement in your writings. Never forget, people are the best judge of your writings. You should always accept criticism in a positive way and utilize to better your writings. You would personally experience after a passage of time that your writings are improved much qualitatively.

Developing writing habits don't necessarily mean that you be a writer. How good it is while being in any profession you could develop simultaneously writing habits too? You are writing something about public motivation towards wellness of the mankind which is going to inspire our youth for a better world. You are in business so you wrote about the trick of business you're professing in and you also discussed about different kinds of risks involved in business. Your small tips regarding business management skills to budding entrepreneurs would be much motivating them. The experiences of your legal profession when converted into book would help out the budding lawyers to overcome the rigors of advocacy. Your writings would be received by your generations with a Big Bang. You will be remembered as a torch bearer for the youth who have to take on the baton from you to complete the big human race. The greatest personal achievement from writing habits is going to be the kind of rare satisfaction you are going to get out of the concentration of mind you have attained. The writings which are going to be most valuable assets for you can't be weighed in terms of money only. Rather you, yourself would prove to be a valuable asset for the mankind on this earth.

*"Thinking is considered to be the best exercise of human mind particularly when your mind is thinking mathematically. For being a good writer you are also supposed to be a good reader of prolific literature of your times. It helps in generating much fruitful thoughts due to confluence of ideas of other best authors of all the times. Kindly welcome criticisms of your conscious readers, when it is accepted positively it triggers further improvement in your writings."*

# 21

## YOU ARE THE WINNER

You are born to win. You are a winner in every walk of your life. No person on this earth is a born winner. To get psychological advantage over the adversary, the winners have tendency to imbibe the kind of confidence in their mind that they are born to win. Who are the winners on this earth? Winners are no different than you or any other person. They are just like you. And you too are just like them. Winners think differently with a mindset which has a winning instinct, even while when they retire to bed in the night. Kindly watch winner's personality from a close spot. Observe their movement and body language. It is quite natural in them what they have mentally practiced. They do not imitate it but they develop an image to be the winner. Watch carefully, you would find that they move like a winner, they walk like a winner, they talk like a winner. Yes…!!! It is.

You may have chosen any field of your liking in your life. It could be a field of medicine, scientific research and business profession, field of law practice and social work or even sports. What makes you the winner? Or what could be the attitude which makes you feel of the winner? Feel a situation when you rein on the top of the world by virtue of your caliber, knowledge and capacity that you do the things in a manner that makes you a unique personality. That's sounds a great argument that no one could be a winner overnight. There is a substance in it. Sure, that would be against the nature. Let us not understand it in terms of winning battles. Winners in battles could not be the winners of human hearts for the reasons of manipulation tactics they adopt to win by any hook or crook. You are born to win, to be the winners of human hearts and rule them on, even after you die. In motivational workshops, I speak on how to win and how to be the winners? While speaking during such workshops it has never been for me unidirectional but was quite interactive. I use to get multiple kind of inspiration from my well informed audience, which pushes me as well to be the ultimate winner in keep doing my sincere efforts for the sake of the mankind on this earth.

Once a very interesting query from the audience was that how come the lions in the jungle are the winner? They are 'born to win' or they are 'born winners'? Oho...!!! Nice. Very good question. Startling indeed. Lions could be the winners? How come? Let me confess that it took me sometime to correlate the things. I responded just spontaneously to the audience, 'all lions are animals, but all animals are not lions'. There was a pleasant silence amongst the audience. It gave me the kind of relief that the audience was able to understand that as to how the lions could not be the winners? It was now logical for me to explain that all human beings are human beings only.

Once you are able to develop within yourself the characteristics of a winner, no force on this earth can stop you from becoming the sure shot winner. See in them, and feel it the kind of madness the winners have, which makes them unstoppable. The tenets for madness to win are that day and night you are thinking nothing but about the goals of your life which you targeted to achieve. You have confined yourself within the four walls of your objectives. Even while you are asleep, you are heard speaking about your winning instinct. You have developed your habit sleeping as a winner in the night, while getting up as a winner in the morning. Make sure, now you are unstoppable. You are the winner. You are born to win. Salute to you. The world is waiting in you, the much awaited winner.

*"That's sounds a great argument that no one could be a winner overnight. Let us not understand it in terms of winning battles. Winners in battle could not be the winners of human hearts for the reasons of manipulation tactics they adopt to win by any hook or crook. You are born to win, to be the winners of human hearts and rule them on, even after you die. Once you are able to develop within yourself the characteristics of a winner no force on this earth can stop you from becoming the sure shot winner."*

---

# 22

## MAKE THINGS HAPPEN

You are regularly making sincere efforts to make the things happen for you. You are very honestly putting in all that what all is required to be done to accomplish your task. On occasions you also work under adverse circumstances. Such adverse circumstances could be of the nature, either incidental or circumstantial which are not within your control. Maybe you find that the things are not happening for you the way you expected. Your disappointment is quite natural. But being disappointed is no remedy for you. As a sensitive man, you need to look for the factors as to why the things didn't happen for you despite your sincere efforts? May be you find no reasons. You are disappointed again. But this is not going to be the solution for you. Not only you but there are a large number of youth like you having similar complaints. Should we consider that they all are serious? Yes…!!! They are all serious and sensitive too. They have assessed about their performances honestly. It is true that sitting silently with their fingers crossed is not going to help out our young masses.

We all work in a system made by us only. Our system works good and satisfactorily provided the stakeholders in the system carry on their responsibilities and accountabilities too. The system fails to produce desired results once the caretakers of system go dishonest and they start working which is prejudicial to the system's interest.

This makes as things do not happen in manner as expected. If it is system's fault that our youth are disappointed, which could be a remote possibility, then it becomes very unfortunate and a matter of grave concern for all of us. Problem in fact starts arising for, we made the system to be controlled by us all through our elected representatives but things happened just opposite, when the system started controlling us. This did not happen in a day or two. It took decades altogether for the system to go so defective and unproductive ultimately. We too remained idle and least concerned about regular deterioration of the system. Now we appear to be worried about since it has started making its direct impact and is adversely affecting our own vested interests. We fail to find any viable way out for its correction because our bonafide are not above board. Concede this fact honestly when you noticed first that your system was going the other way but you kept silent since it did not harm your interests directly. Now the circle is complete and you are directly hit by the system. Now you understand that it was not without reason that despite your sincere efforts you could not succeed.

It becomes the collective responsibility not only of the caretakers but of the stakeholders as well, to see and ensure measures that system works and it facilitates the things to happen so that our youth get expected results in their endeavors. Their disappointment is going to cost very high to the system. Simultaneously, we too would have to make the things happen, not only for us but for our fellow citizens as well. My humble submission would be that now it is not going to be that easy to fight a system which has been allowed to go corrupt for all these decades. Fighting such system from within would be more effective comparatively than fighting that system without. See...!!! That majority of likeminded youth energetic men are able to make entry into the system so as to make the things happen in larger public interest. People honest and dedicated for the nation are the need of the hour. Make things happen for you by taking a lesson from the small spider which even after successive failures has a 'never give it up' attitude and is successful at last in making the web 'system' for itself.

*"We all work in a system made by us only. If it is system's fault, which could be a remote possibility, then it becomes a matter of grave concern for all of us. Our youth in the defective system are getting disappointment for the reasons that despite their sincere efforts they were unable to make things happen the way they expected. We also remained indifferent and let the system go deteriorated. Disappointment of the youth is going to cost very high for the system."*

# 23

## WELCOME ADVERSITIES

Human life is full of adversities with ups and downs. We have got human life so not only we have to justify our existence on this earth but we would have to face any such situation which may adversely affect our initiatives. The man who is moving forward, he would have his chances of being fallen down. The one who is not moving at all, he would have no chances to fall down, but at the same time he would have no chance to reach anywhere. You are a man with determination to reach to the heights of glory in your life by measuring out the limits of sky. So you are in action, you are on move and then why to be worried about it that you would fall down? No doubt, adversities in life are not in good taste. Where the adversities prolong in human life the situation becomes more painful. But you are not the kind of man that you are going to breakdown due to adversities in your life. You are a brave man to conquer adversities and you are not for defeat.

Adversities come in everybody's life without an exception. Consider it as a rule of nature in your life management. Welcome adversities in your life. If you are not facing with adversities then there appears to be something wrong and you are going to miss the most essential phase of your life. Make it a point that you are destined to be a great man, once you are coated with strength of life adversities. Otherwise you must be a surprised man, where you find your life with lesser adversities. You want to leave behind, an imprint of your presence with success on this earth then you would have to welcome adversities instead of getting disheartened. A man who has got birth on this earth he has to die one day. Let your birth be remembered after you die or else let it be lost in oblivion. Choice is yours.

Adversities, like not getting success despite sincere efforts, are of very common nature for us. Always the prevailing circumstances could not be exactly favorable, the way a man expects to be. But still the man has to survive by making the things better for him. We always come across economic adversities in our life. It is impossible in today's world if we do not encounter situations full of adversities. What is the ultimate option left before you? You would be forced by the societal situations, like to mentally prepare yourself and face the adversities head on. Welcome your adversities without getting depressed and heavy hearted when you are convinced that you have to pass through them for your better survival on this earth.

You are a good researcher in science or art. Even after years of concerted research you do not get the desired results. Your getting frustrated is quite obvious. Anyone do. Your entire work for years was going to be null, you feel. Is there no other way out left behind? Achievers are not the ordinary persons. They are born to win, they know it. For them life is not a bed of roses. You are also the one from amongst them. This is a rule of game that everyone who is participating in the race cannot be declared to be the winner. So you have to be there, on top of the win. Keep it in your mind that you are sensitive enough to feel the adversities in your life and you value them. The adversities make you strong from inside to the core of your heart. The hardships around you give you an environment so that you can train yourself tough to even keep working while suffering through the spells of ups and downs. You are a strong man since you welcomed adversities. They are not able to deter you anymore. You are now a fight master ready to play different roles successfully. You keep winning them come what may. You feel that it could be possible of your adversities only.

*"Adversities come in everybody's life without an exception. Consider it as rule of nature in your life management. Welcome adversities in your life. If you are not facing with adversities then there appears to be something wrong and you are going to miss the most essential phase of your life. No doubt, adversities in life are not in good taste but the winners get used to it. Achievers are not the ordinary persons and you are also one amongst them."*

---

# 24

## THE HUMAN TOUCH

We are human beings and we are for the human beings. We have got birth as a human on this earth therefore we have to do acts which are not unbecoming of a human being. Humanism is the kind of human feeling touch which we need to practice for a peaceful and happy world. The human touch does not go for any religion or caste. It has a natural tendency of attachment and attraction for human beings by virtue of the fact that they are born as human, irrespective of any other consideration. Don't you feel that in the present global environment, all is not going well? Where has gone the touch of brotherhood, which we have often preached? We are heard preaching in words but we do not practice in reality. This is cheating to one own self. Why do we feel hatred in the name of caste and creed? What goes wrong if people practice different religions? Why do we distinguish between them as to a man belongs to a particular religion or caste? By virtue of practicing different religions or belonging to different castes, does not mean that they cease to be human beings first.

All religions being practiced on this earth reach to the same destination. They all move to finally search and reach to the blessings of the Almighty. More important is that they could attain the enlightenment so they are blessed with the kind of human touch, to pass on in the service of the mankind. Let the peace and brotherhood prevail on this earth. No religion teaches us to feel hatred with fellow human beings. But why we become so self centered? Who are the human beings? Why do we need to be redefined? That should not be a difficult word to redefine with. Human beings on this earth are the existences with delicate human sensibilities which are controlled and regulated by their mind which is the center of love and passion, gives the logic and reason, with justness and fairness of thoughts and its application. Human beings are distinguished with other creatures only by reason of their logical mind. It becomes an altogether different thing when human logic absolutely goes unfair and unjust. It is deliberate, since it goes malicious with all malafide to cause harm to its own fellow human beings. It could well be stopped if the human mind shuns the malice but persons with ill motives continue to go with it, thereby human suffers missing the very delicate human touch.

Human feelings of pleasure and pain, its expressions and converting it into communicable modes, to help future generations of the mankind to live with peace, are unparallel and are supposed to be the basic components of human sensibilities. Respecting the sentiments of a man with due regard to his feelings or humiliating him without caring for his sentiments, are the two practical dimensions of human behaviors which are ordinarily noticed. One could remain neutral as well, but that is very rare. If you do not feel to respect a man, you have no reasons to humiliate him either. This is the kind of hatred we come across. This is not the feel of a human being. The nature conferred this earth and the environment so that we live with joy and happiness, with a sense of mutual respect. But we have failed to preserve this sensibility and divided this earth into different regions. We have human divisions based upon religion, caste and creed. Why do we allow ourselves to fight with each other based on such divisions? Who instigates us? This is against the humanity and the humanitarian values. We need to identify the perpetrators of human hatred. They would be deterred, only when we come out with firm determination and make them known that they would no more be successful to use us as a tool in their hands for their ulterior motives. We are human beings first and human beings last.

*"The nature conferred this earth and the environment so that we live with joy and happiness with a sense of mutual respect. But we have failed to preserve this sensibility and divided this earth into different regions. We have human divisions based upon religion, caste and creed. All religions practiced on this earth reached to the same destination. We are human beings first and human beings last."*

---

# 25

## POWER OF YOUR THOUGHTS

You will find this in number of literatures that your mind is a powerful machine. It generates such powerful thoughts that on the strength of these thoughts a man can achieve anything in his life whatever he intends to achieve. Today we find that science has achieved unbelievable all around us. This could be possible only because of the ideas and thoughts which originated in the mind of the great scientists of all the time. You want to be an achiever. Sometimes you feel that you are failing in your attempts. You know that you are making sincere and honest efforts. There is no reason to be bogged down with depression and continue with it. The continued phases of depression attempt to overpower you, by completely jamming your cognitive mental faculty. That is dangerous since your mental power to think promptly and logically gets slowly paralyzed by the negative impulses of your depressed mind. Never allow such a phase to arrive at in your life.

See...!!! You cannot avoid depressive phases in your life. It is the bio-chemistry of your mind which is responsible for that. When you feel sad because of your failures, the bio-chemistry of your mind is disturbed, so you feel like that. You come into deep phases of depression for the reasons of secretion and accumulation of such chemicals in your body system which makes you dull and worried. At the same time when you feel pleasant by reasons of your achievements, the bio-chemistry of mind goes very soothing making you feel very happy and cheerful. Such joyful moments activate secretion of chemicals making you feel good. When you are sad, though it is a running phase, the choice before you is that either you continue with it, or try to get rid of it. It is absolutely dependent upon you only. You start reaching to the point of acute depression when you do not find yourself in a position to get yourself out of the depressive stages. You start feeling yourself to be sick. Medicines are not going to help you out. The medical experts will go for therapeutic treatment only because they know that it is not the medicine but it is the power of thoughts in the man which is going to help cure him and bring him out of the depression stage.

The medical science better understands the power of your thoughts. Doctors are seen going with a series of counseling sessions of the man and they try to induce the mind cells so that they start generating powerful positive thoughts in the mind of a man. The vigor of thoughts is experienced by the man throughout his whole body. The body cells start sensing the power of your thoughtful mind and become much more energetic and full of strength. The bio-chemical secretion by these powerful thoughts goes on to neutralize the bio-chemicals released by depressive thoughts. Very soon the man starts feeling good and gets out of his sickness. Your body and the mind completely work upon a well defined bio-chemical actions and reactions. Your thoughts when are dull and negative, your mind is forced to go dull and generate negativity. Once your mind goes dull your body has to be dull and sad. Feel the power of your thoughts and feel the power of confidence in you and in your personality. It is for this reason the great thinkers and motivational writers always recommend that your book shelf must possess sufficient positive literature. You should be a regular reader of such books which give constructive ideas and positive thoughts. Such literature acts as a catalyst to your mind cells and accelerates in them with flow of powerful thoughts. Move with strength. The strength lies in your thoughts.

*"You start feeling yourself to be sick. Medicines are not going to help you out. The medical experts will go for a therapeutic treatment only because they know that it is not the medicine but it is the power of thoughts in the man which is going to help cure him and bring him out of the depression stage. The bio-chemical secretion by powerful thoughts goes on to neutralize the bio-chemicals released by depressive thoughts. Very soon the man starts feeling good and gets out of his sickness."*

# 26

## YOUR FUTURE WAITS

You are out on a mission in your life. May be you have secured your future by getting a job up to your satisfaction but merely getting a job had not been the mission of your life. Your mission in life has been to achieve for others, in addition to what you have achieved for yourself. It also happens that in your life you could not get, the way you wanted your future to be. No problem, every person has a future. Your future does not essentially mean to be your career. You might have seen people who could be successful in their career but they feel to be failures in their life. Why this feeling of failure? One should be content with his career. But he is not content only by his career. Have you ever tried to think that what could be the reason behind? You are born with a mission in your life. Your future waits for you.

There is a famous saying that one should live in present. People are also heard saying, as being uncertain about their future. They say that who knows what is going to happen tomorrow? It is agreed that one should live in present because that is just before you while the future is yet to come. To my thinking, saying that who has seen tomorrow, is blatantly irresponsible statement, in the sense that my today itself is going to lay down the foundation stone for tomorrow. My humble submission is that, if one is honest in his efforts in present, he could know his future. Yes…!!! It could be said with confidence by anyone that your future could either be good or bad, depending upon the nature of your efforts put in by you. Make sure, if your efforts are extraordinary your future too is going to be extraordinary. To be an extraordinary, you need to put some more extra efforts than ordinary. Don't you plan for your future? Yes…!!! You make a plan today keeping in mind, your future. People should make future planning. You are planning in today definitely for a better tomorrow. You surely understand the quality of your planning today. You make a good plan keeping in mind your available resources and also subject to your capacity to work upon.

Planning for future is important. Plan your future with a serious mind. Planning beyond your working capacity would not be fair. Don't compare yourself with others. Believe in your working capacity. You can better develop that through perseverance. Comparing with others would frustrate you. Every person is unique in himself having his individual skills, feel of sensibility and the manner of understanding the things. Every person has his varied individual potential to work. You too can further improve upon. With regular practice of your skills, you will be in a commanding position to shape your future exactly the way you wanted to be. The human achievements are full of illustrations where people's present happened to be quite average but through perseverance their future was much excellent. Had they been lived in present only, they would have continued to be the only average? By living in present they kept thinking about future also. They emerged out excellent. Live in present no doubts. Simply living in present won't serve the purpose unless you are keeping a sharp eye on your future. Keeping thinking about excellent future always makes open scope towards excellence. Again merely thinking won't be enough, work upon it. Your mindset for excellence regularly inspires you to work. Once there are inputs of a concrete future plan it become easier for your working mind to come out with best outputs. You would see future is waiting for you which would be an excellent future indeed.

*"Every person has a future. You are born with a mission in your life. Your future awaits you. You have to be extraordinary so you plan your present accordingly. Planning for future is important. Plan your future with a serious mind. Planning beyond your working capacity would not be fair. Do not compare yourself with others. Believe in your working capacity. You can better develop that through perseverance. Comparing with others would frustrate you. Keep thinking about excellent future always makes open scope towards excellence,"*

# 27

## EXPRESS YOUR KNOWLEDGE

You are a knowledgeable man, it reflects in your personality and body language. The world so recognizes you, by getting your well communicative expressions either in written form or through words of your mouth. Do we intend to say that being recognized by people from the world would be essential? If the world fails to recognize your knowledge then your wisdom would be of no meaning. So being self content with knowledge is not enough? Do not think like this that world failed to recognize your knowledge but take it this way that you failed in properly expressing your knowledge to the world. Once your expression of knowledge is mixed with its practical applications then it acquires and attracts much wider dimension of people's attention and the world gets ready to welcome you.

This is a settled fact that knowledge is power. You happen to write an examination, naturally with an objective to pass that examination with good ranks. May be you feel yourself to be good with knowledge but you are not going to evaluate your answer sheet. It would be evaluated by some other person who is supposed to be an expert in the subject. He awards you marks much below your calculated expectations. You become disappointed by the lesser marks you have been awarded. You show your resentment that your answer sheet is not evaluated properly. The system comes out with its inability to help you. You do not get any satisfactory reply either. Now the question arises, who says that you are a knowledgeable person? That would be your assessment about your knowledge but the system finds you much below that. You can't help. You have qualified written examination and have been called for an interview before a body of experts. The experts are expected to assess the suitability of your knowledge and personality for a particular job you have applied for. The expert body does not found you suitable for that post and your candidature has been rejected. You feel much aggrieved about it. You were content with your knowledge but what went wrong? You are correct that you passed written examination by virtue of your knowledge only. People also do consider that written examination had been very tough, the one you cleared. But now the truth is that you have been rejected by the experts during your interview, despite the fact that you possessed knowledge. The expert body did not recognize your knowledge. It goes to show that feeling yourself content with knowledge is not enough unless the world would so recognize your knowledge. That is possible when you possess expression and communicative skills of your knowledge.

Now you are in a position to conclude that communicating your knowledge is more significant than possession of your knowledge. Today is an era of advertisements. You also advertise yourself for best appreciation of your knowledge. Consumer markets are full of products but without proper advertisement they do not get big number of customers. People would be able to value, once you successfully express your knowledge. In job markets our youths are fighting very hard in search for a suitable employment. Equally the employers are also in search of knowledgeable minds. Always keep this positive orientation that during any selection committee for an appointment, the interviewers are not sitting to reject you in the interview but they are sitting there to select you, by cross checking your knowledge. Now it is up to you that you are presenting yourself nicely by means of fully communicating your knowledge and convincing them to select you. They are there to appreciate your knowledge. Recognition of your knowledge by others is important in a world of competition.

All the best to you. Move ahead with confidence because you know that you have the knowledge. Let others also know your wisdom.

*"Communicating your knowledge is more significant than your possessing it. Today is an era of advertisements. Advertise yourself for best appreciation of your knowledge. People would be in a position to value your knowledge once you are successfully expressing your knowledge."*

---

# 28

## NO NEGATIVE THOUGHTS

In its practicality it would be not that easy to define negative thinking. In the sense that what you think is positive to your outlook but your opponents may declare your thinking to be absolutely negative. Therefore, without bothering for what others say, it is to be understood in relative sense. Normally people are in the habit of criticizing others just for the sake of criticism. Thus, criticizing itself is a negative approach particularly when people are not honest, and intend to find fault with others. Life itself is full of trials and errors. Mistakes are quite natural. Err is to human. The positive dimension of human personality must be that instead of finding fault with others, one should help in rectifying other's mistakes. Human personality has its own limitations. No person on this earth can claim for sure that he is not prone to errors.

It is always a positive sign that a person commits mistake since he works. He takes initiatives and then he learns out of his mistakes to further improve upon, not to repeat again. Those who are not working at all, there is no occasion for them to commit errors. It would be a complete negative thinking approach where a person is always scared of committing mistakes therefore he decides to play safe and not to work upon anything. No work, then no mistakes. This is not the way. There are good numbers of people in society to scare and discourage you. Any negative thinking in the opinion of others could be a complete positive step in your point of view. Never be worried about failures in your life. Thinking about failures is again going to be a negative thought. Remember that great success stories on this earth are born out of a series of failures. Failures become the foundation stones of your ultimate successes. Now the point is that what kind of success you need in fact? It absolutely depends upon your thinking whether you want a success on big scale or else you are content with what you are getting through small pieces of success. Neither you are able to enjoy it nor are you able to quantify it. Decision is absolutely yours. When you become conscious about it then much time has been lost and you find yourself to be nowhere. Now even if you wish to work, you will do it half heartedly where success would not be guaranteed to that scale.

You must be surprised to read as to how come success could be guaranteed one? No one can state like it. Yes…!!! But I have no confusion to repeat about my considered understanding that success is guaranteed provided you make your every step with a determined mind and without any reflection of negativity either in your thoughts or in your personality. Always be confident within yourself that you will act like a winner and think like a winner. Losses are an integral part of everyone's life. You happen to lose many things only to gain lot many things. Never be bogged down by negativities in your way of life's struggles. It could be full with failures, ups and downs, disappointments, discouragements, but you have to be never disheartened. Even manmade adversities would be engineered in your way by your opponents to break you down. Don't bother again. Such times are your testing times. Let your opponents do what they can do. You remain content with positivity without any negativity against them. Be sure, they cannot do more than that what they are doing. You don't have any time to think about them or their misdeeds. You have no time to think of seeking any revenge from them either. You have to think about yourself only and your targets. Your negative thinking will harm you only, make it a point. Success for you is guaranteed this way because you are pursuing nothing but your life objectives with a positive mindset.

*"But I have no confusion to repeat about my considered understanding that success is guaranteed provided you make your every step with a determined mind and without any reflection of negativity either in your thoughts or in your personality. Never be bogged down by negativities in life. You happen to lose many things only to gain lot many things. Life itself is full of trials and errors. Your failures become foundation stones of your ultimate success."*

---

# 29

## LET PEOPLE EXPLORE YOU

Your attitude in your life's mission is very significant. It reflects your self-confidence and firm determination to catch your mission. You become so packed with your goals that on occasions you feel lost within yourself. On many occasions your next step could be absolutely unpredictable to others. They may not be able to understand you as to what kind of person you are? Be sure that when you are confident about your next steps and other future line of actions, then you should not at all be bothered about people's reaction. Let them to explore you. You are on route to your mission without making much propaganda about it. Sharing of thoughts is good but such sharing all the time, to all the people could prove to be damaging to your future plans. It should be exclusively your decision based upon your assessments, as to with whom you are going to rely upon to share with your plans. While executing your plans you need only the most trusted friends so that you can go one successfully giving them responsibilities to work upon your plan. Such people could be very few, who could be trusted and made your fellow strugglers.

I was talking about your attitude. It's a tendency of mind with your confidence and determination studded tough deep within your personality which reflects in your day to day performances. You walk with an attitude in your movement and even while you talk and smile with an attitude. Your expressions and eye-to-eye communication capacities are so unique that your attitudinal responses reach deep to the hearts at the receiving ends. To be a successful man one needs to have an attitude. It is my personal observation that society does not like your attitude. Your attitude becomes a long mission of your life and you forget rest of the unnecessary things happening around you. When you are moving with determination to reach up to your objectives people jealous to you would look to your weaknesses to pull you down. They do not like your attitude for the reasons best known to them. It could be their inferiority complex. But you cannot help it out. No one on this earth could be said to be perfect. Human weaknesses are there and you cannot be an exception to that. You always work with an attitude that human weaknesses could be won over. Human errors and mistakes in good faith are excusable. If you are working with command you will be the person who could control your weaknesses.

Historical testimonies reveal that one can become an easy victim, being trapped by his weaknesses which are engineered by his opponents. Every person may have his own weaknesses. Falling prey to their traps becomes possible when your weaknesses become very common and known to everybody. Human weaknesses are very common. Your opponents keep exploring your antecedents. In the first instance, it is advisable that by making honest endeavors, you should win over your weaknesses. May be without your knowledge you were made prey to some mistakes which you could have never done consciously. When you are honest situations are going to help you. By conscious care and precautions you can definitely ensure that you don't fall prey to any trap laid by your opponents and your weaknesses are minimized to a considerable extent. You will be thus able to establish winning attitude for yourself. Mistakes done in good faith are justifiable through logic which your opponents even cannot counter. Let them explore your weaknesses. Keep them busy exploring you. You keep moving exploring your winning attitudes.

*"Attitude is a tendency of mind with your confidence and determination studded tough deep within your personality which reflects in your day to day performances. You walk with an attitude and even talk and smile with an attitude. Your attitudinal expressions and communication capacities are superb. Human weaknesses are very common. Consciously ensure that you do not fall prey to the traps laid by your opponents. Let them explore your weaknesses. Keep them busy exploring you."*

---

# 30

## ATTEND YOUR KIDS

Look to your small and cheerful family, naughty lovely kids. They need your close caring and attention while you are in pursuit of your life objectives. Charity begins at home that you should remember. You have to ensure on top priority that your kids are not left uncared and unattended. Your family is the first investment for you then comes the society where you would be investing later. You have to spare time from your busy engagements, for love and affection to your family and the kids. While they are kids they need your special attention. Even while they grow young they keep looking for your support. A child has the best learning mind and capacity to catch things which are taught to him. What they are made to learn in their childhood, it lasts in their mind till they live. It is your individual liability to feed your children, with great thoughts and good habits. Remember, that your kids are the best images of yours. In them and in their faces, you see your image. You are here to live again, in the shape of your kids.

May be you are having a lot of works to do. You have your own life objectives. Your kids are also well included in your life objectivities. You are so content with your objectives that you do not find much time for other work. You are hiring services of other people, to assist you in your work. This way you are not able to find time to attend to your family and the kids. They feel neglected, although you are not doing it intentionally. The kids might not have developed much maturity of understanding but the child psychology demands that they need your constant grooming touch right from their infancy and childhood. You have no reason to compromise with this situation, at the cost of psychological development of your kids. You have to find time for your kids from your tight busy schedule.

Whatever career you are pursuing with, it is good that you intend to be on top of your career. You can do it, only with a constant peace of mind. Your peace of mind starts from your home. If the home environment is disturbed, since you have no time for your kids, then make sure that you will not be able to achieve your targets in your life the way you wanted. You will find one day that the best learning period for your kids, to learn good habits has been passed away because you did not care about it. They learnt bad habits. They have gone out of control, by the time gradually they became young. Now it is too late for them and you as well. You are feeling much painful. The peace of your home is gone. You cannot say that you are not affected by it. But you find that you are not able to help you out. I have personally come across such instances that people neglected their kids. They remained busy with their work in earning money by whatever means. By the time the children deviated from their rightful path. You need to avoid any such situation in your life because it is going to defeat you in your life. Kindly take out some time from your busy schedule and invest this time with your children exclusively. In between their study days, take them for outings to some places full with natural beauty. Let them see the nature around and have interaction with it, so that they come with creative mind. Always nourish them with positive ideas, so as to make them responsible while they become young and are ready to face the outside world. You also inculcate in them, to be ready to face the worldly challenges. That would be enough for you and you can feel satisfied yourself along with your kid's future and content with peace of your mind to pursue your life objectivities in its totality.

*"A child has the best learning mind and capacity to catch things which are taught to him. What they are made to learn in their childhood it lasts in their mind till they live. It is your individual liability to feed your children with great thoughts and good habits. Always nourish them with positive ideas so as to make them to face worldly challenges. Remember that your kids are the best images of yours. In them and in their faces you see your image. You are here to live again in the shape of your kids."*

---

# 31

## DO NOT BLAME

Finding fault with others or making people responsible for others mistakes is not considered to be a positive human behavior. It could be usually noticed that people find faults very easily but when they are asked to rectify such faults then they fail to come out with any suggestive measures. In whatever profession you are, depending upon group activity, you have distributed your work among other members of the group. Your expectation is that they should perform the allotted work the way you wanted. They are making their efforts honestly to the best of their capacity and understanding but they fail up to your expectations. May be it was due to their lack of expertise and experience. They could not come up with the desired results within the specified time limit or even if they happen to come out with some results, it is not found to be of up to the mark. You lost your control all of the sudden and started shouting at them. Your subordinates get disappointed. They look at you feeling sorry about it. They want to speak to you to explain with certain points. You are not ready to listen to them and kept blaming for all that.

Similar could be your behavior for others who are not known to you. Take it that those who are subordinate to you, they are going to digest your behavior but others may not because they are not your subordinates. There is every possibility that they are going to raise objections against you. Blaming others for no reasons is not fair. It means making certain allegations without any justifiable cause. You could be right sometimes while blaming others. But this would be absolutely unfair when you jump to certain conclusions without affording the other person a reasonable opportunity to be heard. You need to listen to the defenses of the other person before reaching to any conclusion and declaring the act of the person to be blameworthy. This would be unfair in the sense that you are hurting the feeling of the other person. That is true that you have every authority to possess your own pattern of thinking and to behave with others. But at no stage, the human consciousness authorizes you to play with the sentiments of others, that too without any proof for making such blame. Did you try to look for the compelling circumstances of other man which were beyond his control? Due to those circumstances he would have lost his control over his actions. Had such compelling circumstances not been there such omission would not have taken place? Once you are keeping all these situations in mind your behavioral approach is always going to be right and others do not feel like to be objectionable.

You see, your subordinate was not able to give you the result the way you wanted. You are a professional so you should behave like a professional. Don't shout at him. Instead of putting him into the docks try to understand the problem he is facing with and then guide him accordingly with all patience. If you so find, still do not blame him provided he is honest and reform him by putting him with proper training schedule. You will find that very soon he is able to give the results you wanted, quite efficiently. Off course, if he is found to be careless, not properly concentrating to the work then you have every reason to take notice of it and act accordingly. Being professional is very important in the sense that you should not tolerate any intentional act or omission. At the same time respecting the human values is also a significant part of your professionalism.

*"Blaming others for no reason is not fair. You could be right sometimes blaming others. But this would be absolutely unfair when you jump to certain conclusions without any show cause. Your professionalism requires that you need to practice such values with your subordinates. His honest mistakes need reformation initiatives on your part at the same if he acts foul deliberately then your professionalism requires that he should be taken to task. Remember that respecting human values is equally professional."*

---

# 32

## HAVE DREAMS

You dream first, and then pursue your dreams. Dreaming is by human nature. They are the foundations of your life success. We talk about day dreaming which we use to see with our eyes open. We not only dream when we are asleep but we also dream while we are awake. Dreaming is not bad, but not doing anything for fulfillment of your dreams is bad. You dream big, so that you can achieve big. Dreaming big and dreaming difficult are two different dimensions but they are interdependent. If you choose to dream big but avoid seeing the difficult, there is every possibility that you are not going up to achieve your dreams. People keep passing comments that the dreams are dreams only and do not come out to be true. You see dreams while you are sleeping but when you wake up; you find that it was all false. Dreams then simply prove to be illusions. People may also ridicule your day dreaming. Your question should be as to what is wrong in day dreaming? At least in day dreaming one is dreaming with his eyes open. You dream to be a big scientist, a popular political leader, a good sportsman, a Nobel laureate or a great human being.

Where you dream to be a Nobel laureate, you are that, make your dreams to be the foundation behind fulfilling your dreams. The stronger the foundation, more determined you are to reach up to your dreams and to work for it. When you understand to mean to be a Nobel laureate then you also know the kind of efforts to be put in, to be the Nobel laureate. You are supposed to be on top of your knowledge regime when the world recognizes you by conferring with Nobel Prize. Being on top of knowledge is not every body's game, the world also understands it. In making your dreams come true it was neither an overnight job, nor was to be achieved within few months or years. You worked rigorously day and night, for decades and decades altogether then only you emerged as knowledge impersonate. You remain so content with your work that you forget about, if you dreamt to be a Nobel laureate. The world is running after you to recognize you and to designate you a Nobel laureate. Now after working for all these decades you have become so polite that you feel no sensation to be a winner of Nobel Prize.

Scientists or sports persons are not made in a day or two. It takes decades to be a world class scientist. There were occasions when experimenting scientists could not get results. He was about to lose his balance. He controlled himself but he never lost his working determination to perform. He also had a dream to rule the world so they had to be world class. He dreamt to be an Olympian. It takes decades to be a world class sportsperson who spent youth of their life with rigorous practice on the ground. Once a sportsperson happens to miss his medal in Olympics, he has to wait for the next four years targeting for his medal again, with the same rigorous schedule for years. He is targeting for gold medal. If he would not dream for it, how would he work on it? He will keep working untiring till he achieves his dreams. Right from the day one, he practices regularly for all those four years rigorously without a single break. You need to be constantly in sound physical and mental health for carrying on such hard practices so as to realize your dreams. You will be in that state of mind when you are thinking big and positive. Winners are those who never let loose. History of the winners has been testimony to this fact that they had been great dreamers. Dreams are for you and you are for the dreams.

*"You dream to be a Nobel laureate. It takes decades to be a world class scientist or an Olympian. In making your dreams come true it was neither an overnight job nor was to be achieved within few months or years. Being on top of the world is not every body's game. You worked rigorously for decades only to emerge as knowledge impersonate. Keep it in your mind that so as to realize your dreams; you need to be constantly in sound physical and mental health to practice hard and tough. Dreams are for you and you are for the dreams. Come on...!!!"*

---

# 33

# YOUR INNER WORLD

Your outer world around you in which you live, could be an artificial one full with negativity and jealousness. It is outward social order in which people of varied kind of thinking reside. It is not always necessary that they would be of similar thinking order at par with you. You may not like to control that order and waste your time because you have lot many things in your mind to do for the rest of the world. You have a vast inner world of your own which is within you. This inner world could not be artificial and is the real world of you. It firmly controls your all actions within and without. Have you ever tried to see your inner world and roam around? Think about yourself with your eyes closed and peaceful mind. Take at least one hour out of your daily busy schedule. Sit in a serene atmosphere and allow your inner mind to set in. Assess your actions what you did yesterday, the actions which are in your mind and your plan for today. Also give a thought to your activities for tomorrow. Many of the acts you did yesterday, you may find that your inner conscience is not ready to endorse it. Now what you need to do? You just do not ignore the voice of your inner conscience. Every person has a strong inner conscience. It always signals against your wrongful acts of the day provided you are sensitive enough to receive and respond to those signals.

We human beings cannot claim ourselves to be perfect one in all respects. But at the same time we may come across multidimensional activities in our day to day lives. Thus committing mistakes is quite natural for us but what is objectionable is that even when our wrongful acts come to our notice, we do not stop and still keep repeating that. We deliberately overlooked the inner signals and did an act which our inner world was not permitting. As a result our inner world gets weakened for the reasons of deliberate ignoring and repetitions of wrongful acts on our part. Now who is to be blamed for your weak inner world? You have to carry on lot many tasks and that would not be possible once you go weak. Do you know what is going to happen by weakening of your inner world? You are getting weak gradually, which you should not at any cost. Your inner world which is inside you is a constant source of strength for you. Would you like to be a weak person? You would be able to face the challenges of your outer world strongly, only when you have protected your inner world carefully and have timely responded to its calls, to make it strong. You have assessed your actions of the day. You took a pledge that you would not allow repeating previous errors. You are firmly acting upon it. Sooner you would start getting the results and feel strong from within.

According to the studies in human psychology your inner world is very sensitive, just and fair. It never induces you to do any wrongful act. It is always to protect you and take care of you, provided you do not ignore it. What I mean to ignore, is that on occasions you might have observed when you are out to do something wrong, your inner world always persuades you, to not to do that wrongful act. We take a lot of time to recognize it, by the time it is too late. Your body, your mind, your heart, your sensual organs are the most integral parts of your inner world. They have the natural capacity to take genuine stands unaffected by the outer world. But you need to constantly get trained accordingly in due consonance of your inner world to feel the strength inside you. Practice it; you will be the master of your world.

*"You have a vast inner world of your own within you. It is the constant source of your inner strength by which you are able to face the challenges and hardships of the outer world. Take out some time from your busy schedule to think about yourself with your eyes closed and peaceful mind. You just do not ignore the voice of your inner conscience. Every person has a strong inner conscience. It always signals against your wrongful acts of the day provided you are sensitive enough to receive and respond to those signals before it is too late."*

———————————————————

# 34

## DO NOT FEAR PUBLIC SPEECH

You have good leadership qualities. Look to the history you would find that good leadership used to be good orators. With the help of good speech the speakers directly connect with the people and communicate with them deep to their heart and mind. Thus oratory capacity is most significant component of good leadership. Do not fear making public speeches. Delivering public speech is a nice art. In the beginning it makes a kind of fear in your mind but you should have a never to give up approach. It is developed gradually with the passage of time and by keep on practicing it, as and when one finds an opportunity to address any public meeting. Fearing public speech is a psychological human nature. Keep talking to friends is completely different then making a speech to any gathering. While talking to your friends you feel to be at ease but making public speech at the same time you have to be very informal and attentive. A smooth fluency is noticed in your speech and at the same time catching the attention of your audience when your mind is pregnant with knowledge. Delivery part of your speech making is also equally significant. There could be possibilities of interaction with spontaneous queries from the audience. It would be presence of your mind and the kind of versatile knowledge which will enable you to attend to those queries.

Knowledge being all powerful inculcates within you the kind of confidence to fight out the fear consciousness of public speech. It empowers you to speak without any hitch. For good and impressive speech it is always to be kept in mind that one should possess authentic quality information to deliver with. Cheap category of contents in your speech may go to lose your quality audience. Why one fears about public speech? Did you ever apply your mind about it? First stage of fear arises out of lack of needed confidence for public speech. It is because you are not prepared for it. You do your preparation well so that to mitigate the fear from your mind. Even if you were well informed in advance, you also made necessary preparation for that, but at the time of delivering public speech, you were not able to come out and speak properly for psychological reasons and hesitation. It so happens to everybody in the beginning. Do not consider it to be your weakness. You sensed that your heart beat was increased. You were not able to control yourself and hold the ground properly. You do not find words to come out of your mouth. You feel that your mind all of a sudden has gone empty with no ideas. You failed in expressing and communicating yourself. Some of the words you remember while lot many words you are forgetting with your heart beats up. You are now disappointed. Disappointment triggers fear, which is quite human. But you have not to fear at all and have to counter your fear with a regular practice on this front. In the beginning, for everyone public speech may appear to be fearful but gradually you will find that you have developed that needed confidence in you with the passage of time and you are now among good orators of your times.

Always remember disappointment is an integral part of human life. From behind the shadows of disappointments, emerge the rays of hope. Getting fear is quite natural but you should not. Disappointments give you the needed strength to muster the courage and fight under adverse circumstances. What you need to do is to improve your public speech by selection of proper words with good informative contents which better communicate to the audience. Proper pronunciation of words is equally significant. Defective pronunciation hampers your all hard work with defective communication. So you have to be very careful about it that a good orator is always a good communicator.

*"At the time of public speech you felt that your heart beat was increased. You were not able to hold the ground properly. You do not find words to come out of your mouth. You feel that your mind suddenly has gone empty with no ideas. You failed in expressing and communicating yourself. You are now disappointed. Disappointment triggers fear."*

# 35

## FOCUS YOUR TARGETS

Life without any objective or target is of no use. It is just like animals live up their life and die ultimately. Can you survive in your life without target, whether big or small? You cannot because you will feel that your life without objectives had no meaning. A life which was left behind without meaning would be a life spent like animal life. We are expected to make our life worth living. We need to draw a mission for our life with pious objectives. Keeping the life objectives in mind now fix your targets in order to reach those targets one by one, in accordance with your working capacity. On the bigger canvass of life objectives you have to paint through the dots of your systematic targets. Do not make a target just for the sake of it. It is kind of cheating and is going to harm you at different life stages. We all have different working capacity to perform. So fixing of targets could be lesser or bigger subject to individual capacity to perform. It has been noticed that people make life targets beyond their capacity to work. Ultimately they fail to reach up to their targets for obvious reasons. Disappointment is bound to settle down in them. Please avoid this. In whatever field you are, you should always aspire to excel and to be on top of the world. Thinking to be on top could be easy but achieving that sort of excellence could be a very tough task. Friends always target to be world class.

How to choose your target completely depends upon your aptitude and temperament. It so happens that targets are imposed upon you against your will in which you are not interested. Try to see that you have a freedom of choice while fixing your targets. Always be selective in it otherwise overlapping ideas do not give rise to the needed clarity about your target. Carefully made targets are very easy to achieve provided you are making your move in a well planned and systematic manner. You honestly assess yourself first with an open mind and about the nature of your targets you are aiming for. One concentrates with complete dedication provided he is proceeding as per his likings. You need to see that your targets are not merely imaginary but they are based upon sound considerations. Do not think beyond your capacity otherwise you will fail. Successive failures are sufficient to destroy your focusing capacity of mind. That's the caution, because at the time you work to achieve your targets you have to simultaneously focus yourself so accurately that once you decided to hit the target, you hit that.

Fixing targets is not going to yield any result to you unless you pursue your targets with a focused mind. Focusing your targets mean when you are going to concentrate for your target, you see nothing but your target. Despite busy surroundings, you remember your target only. Reaching up to the stage of focused mind is a difficult task but not impossible. This stage could only be achieved through perseverance. There are lot many worldly situations existing around you which are sufficient to divert your attention. Such disturbing situations may come up one after the other making it very difficult for you to focus your mind to the target. You may come across number of family problems as well. You cannot ignore your family problems while keeping your concentration for the target intact. Agreed...!!! That is very difficult exercise. Read life history of great men that despite adversities in their life they kept struggling tough with their mind focused and were able to achieve their targets.

*"On the bigger canvass of life objectives you have to paint through the dots of your systematic targets. Fixing of targets*

*could be smaller or bigger depending upon individual capacity to perform. Always be selective in your targets otherwise overlapping ideas do not give rise to the needed clarity about your targets. It is the aptitude and your temperament to work which would be the decisive factor to select your target and focus accordingly. It is through perseverance that one attains focused mind. Carefully made targets are very easy to achieve provided you are making your move in a well planned and systematic manner."*

---

# 36

## DISCOVER YOURSELF

Read the history of human civilizations and its development from time immemorial. It has been a constant and progressive history from primitive to much more diversified forms of development in human history. There are instances of conflicts also just in a bid to establish supremacy over the other. However, by and large the human mind has been innovative. By its nature it looks for the ways and means to protect and ensure welfare of the people on this earth. It keeps thinking, it writes, makes experiments and goes for smaller to bigger discoveries to the extent of complicated developments through science and technology. These discoveries have all been utilized in the larger welfare of human beings not only for their socio-economic progress but even individually for their increased longevity. Comforts of these discoveries could be enjoyed by upper strata due to their economic soundness but mass human population has not been benefited by these discoveries for the reasons of their poverty conditions, perpetual societal and economic disparities. This has proved to be the saddest part of human civilizations.

Discover yourself in the sense that despite progress of human civilizations, a large portion of human population has been deprived of basic minimum necessities. You discover yourself the avenues which can help you out enabling you to do something for the betterment of such a large deprived populations. Self-discovery may sound to be a very typical word in the sense that discovery for self-development of a person. Have you ever tried to discovered yourself? Self-discovery denotes to that you are trying to understand the purpose of your birth on this earth. Why you came on this earth? Whether you kept thinking about yourself and your near and dears only? You find no time to think about those who are in need of some help in the society. This is true that it is not your liability to help them. But don't you have moral obligations towards your fellow citizens? No doubt that it is government's job to attend to them. But when the governments are failing and getting worthless for public welfare then please do not expect anything from them. Your sensitivity would motivate you to discover yourself. This discovery would take you to the path of humanism. You will find that you have discovered yourself. You are doing for welfare of the people without waiting for what governments do. It is true that you are not that resourceful as compared to the governments but you have that honest enthusiasm to perform which makes all the difference.

Once you have taken the determined step towards self-discovery then always feel the strength of Almighty within you. You have enough with you to satisfy your needs and sufficiently to help others. There is no limit of the greed of a person. It ultimately destroys him. In present days of lies and cheatings, being honest is a very difficult task. Honesty being the best policy, today appears to have lost and become a philosophy of the gone days. But there should be no reason for you to be disappointed. For a person of your temperament honesty only is going to be your strength since you are not in the habit of telling lies and cheating others. Be honest, be human. The day you are able to discover that you are content within yourself you would find that your self-discovery is complete. You have discovered that real inner strength to move forward which no force on this earth can stop. Despite all your scarcities if you are genuinely making your efforts for the sake of the human beings you have lived up to your purpose behind your birth.

*"For a person of your temperament honesty only is going to be your strength since you are not in the habit of telling lies or cheating others. Your sensitivity would motivate you to discover yourself. This discovery would take you to the path of humanism. You will find that you have discovered yourself. You discover those avenues which can help you out enabling you to do something for the betterment of such a large deprived populations. You are doing for welfare of the people without waiting for what governments do."*

---

# 37

## HELPING OTHERS

Thanks to the Almighty that you are fortunate enough to live your life simply and in a best possible manner. You are highly grateful to the Almighty that with whatever little you have, you are most satisfied with. You are able to get your bread and butter, and sound sleep in the nights. You always pray Him that give, only that which fulfills your needs and with the rest you can help others too. What else you want? One keeping himself satisfied with his small possessions is a very difficult task. It is very common that persons getting greedy very often are human weakness. People who are sufficiently rich too have lust for money. Great are the people who spend to help others out of their hard earned money. Make your kids too, like you and train them right from their childhood for simple living and high thinking. Always try to inculcate in you and in your children as well, the habit of self-satisfaction and being content with what they have. Getting with greed is easier but continuing with greed is rather very difficult and demoralizing too. Make them that they do not suffer from feeling of greed and do not expect to get anything, without making sincere and honest efforts. Make your children understand that they should always be ready to help others and believe in giving others rather than taking. This would be a habit which is going to make you enjoy with full pleasure and happiness in your life.

Who helps others? Why to help others? How comes the feeling to help others? There is a very emotional story. A man was sitting in his house and was just getting ready for his dinner. His wife comes with dinner and serves to him. The moment he was about to eat, a man starving for many days, comes to him with his folded hands and stood before him. He requested the man for some food to eat, as he was without food for many days. The man asked his wife to bring some food but there was no extra food in the house. Left with no other option before him and with a bonafide intention to feed the hungry man, the man gave half of his food to him. In the meantime another man approached, he was also hungry and requested for food. The man without any hesitation gave half of his food to the starving man. Both the hungry persons went away after eating food, feeling obliged for the man and offering him their best wishes. The man ultimately went to sleep without food since his wife knew that there was nothing left behind in the house to cook for him again. The wife too went without food with sleepless night.

What is the moral of this story? How many people are going to endorse this kind of helping attitude to others? Some of them may say that it was an extreme instance of helping others. Before understanding the moral of this story, we need to look the morality itself. Who is bothered today to be moral and practice the morality? The society today has gone completely self-centered. Earning money by whatever means has become the sole consideration and respectable in materialistic world. Emotions have changed, parameters are destroyed. They feel more satisfied by keep earnings money rather than helping others. This cannot be said to be moral by any standard. Nobody cares by your moral values or any such set standards. But mind it, that satisfaction is not going to be realistic and is short lived. You follow your rules without discouraging yourself that moral standards in the present society are getting deteriorated. The satisfaction and the emotional touch you are going to get by helping others you will feel that to be spiritual and real. Keep intact your emotions. Your intentions must be pious.

*"Keeping one satisfied with his small possessions is a very difficult task. People who are sufficiently rich too have lust for money. You follow your rules without discouraging yourself that moral standards in the present society are getting deteriorated. Always try to inculcate in you and in your children as well, the habit of self-satisfaction and being content with what they have. Make your children understand that they should always be ready to help others and be happy in life."*

---

# 38

## PRACTICE VIRTUES

In any phase of our life, virtues for us are very significant. Life virtues give us the moral strength to move with our head high. Who likes to move with his head down? Practicing virtues like speaking the truth and the honesty being on top of any human behavioral policy are the best to follow up in any part of time. Naturally we also need to see, if the virtues are going to help us any way. It could only be seen by bringing them into our habits and then observing minutely its impact in our life. It could be an obvious question, which may come to your mind. Whether it is in any manner compulsory for human beings to practice virtues? How does it is going to make any difference if we do not follow the human virtues? Let me submit before you very politely that virtues are for human and human are for virtues which distinguish them from animal existence. We are human beings so we are expected to behave which is not unbecoming of a human being. Human like behavior results ultimately in the form of human values otherwise it will be animal like behavior. Nobody is going to compel you to practice virtues unless your own inner conscience does so. The day you are able to understand your value behind human existence you will go for virtues only. Nobody can scare you unless you are so scared of. You are scared that you have wasted your human life for your wrongs devoid of virtues.

Virtues are not to be practiced in life once in a blue moon. Virtues are your daily behavioral patterns while you perform human interactions among your fellow human beings. Daily one way or the other you happen to come in contact with your fellow human beings. So on every day basis you have to take all care and precautions that you do not forget to practice virtues in your behavior. This universe is of either human beings or of animals and rest is the nature. The human virtues could be embraced not only for fellow human beings but for animals and towards the nature as well. Let the honesty be your virtue. Do you ever feel that whether you are honest to yourself? To whom you are cheating then? To yourself...!!! Strange then...!!! Whether you speak the truth, only when situations so demand? Who knows this better if you are speaking the truth? If you are telling lies, you are the best person to know that you are a liar. Who else...!!! Experience the guilty sense of your mind when you are aware that you are not speaking the truth. Feel your increasing heart beat which you are attempting to suppress down. Yes...!!! You feel it. What does it indicate? That your body and your mind resist that but you are deliberately suffocating the inner voice of your heart. You go on speaking lies despite your body and mind does not allow for that. You are gone with your virtues with lesser happiness in your life.

There is every freedom of choice with you to decide to be honest in your life and not to tell lies. You only compelled yourself to not to speak the truth by going completely against the wishes of your heart and the mind. While speaking the truth and practicing the honesty then you feel the freshness of your mind and pleasant rhythm of your heart beat. You remain strong and healthy. My humble submission would be that be strict to your virtues, nobody can put you down. Never go against the wishes of your heart and the mind. These two organs of your body are the best regulators and the best indicators for your virtues. Be responsive to them and be full of virtues.

*"Let me submit before you very politely that virtues are for human and human are for virtues which distinguish them from animal existence. Nobody is going to compel you to practice virtues*

*unless your inner conscience does so. The universe is of either human beings or of animals and rest is the nature. The human virtues could be embraced not only for fellow human beings but for animals and towards the nature as well. Let the honesty be your virtue. Let the truth prevail. Then you feel the freshness of your mind and pleasant rhythm of your heart beat."*

---

# 39

## AFTER YOUR DEATH

You have taken birth on this earth. You are going to die one day for sure. You have to enjoy your life while you live. Nobody has seen the happenings after your death. The name and fame you have earned that only is going to stay behind when this world would remember your contributions done towards the betterment of this world. The money and other properties you left behind could best be utilized for pious objectives provided it is in worthy hands. It could be seen as very common that people are scared of death. Who wants to die? Despite the fact everybody knows that death is certain for everyone but we fear of it. Death never discriminates among individuals, whether rich or poor, big or small. When death is certain then instead of fearing it, we should do such deeds which leave a legacy behind when we depart from this world. That should be the purpose of our life objectivity. Keep yourself ready to leave behind the legacy after your death. Are you ready for that? Yes…!!! That's the way. You understand that you are the beautiful and best creation of your parents on this earth. Your parents are the real Gods for you. Who is going to suffer most with pain when you die? Your parents are going to be most affected. Their heart will cry out since you are gone, never to come again. Who is there to console them? Nobody can console them at the cost of your life. That is going to be the life for your parents after your death.

This could be one of the scenarios but still. One has to be strong since life is like this only. It is not within the control of your parents otherwise they could have saved you by sacrificing their life. Oh…!!! The Almighty…!!!

After your death, who else is going to cry for you? Your family and the kids are the worst sufferers. There are the people who die before they could live properly. This is all as philosophical as you think it to be. The life is understood but the mystery behind death remains conspicuous, particularly in case of the deaths before age. Approaching towards death is a smooth development of biological cells up to a certain limit which one could quantify as an age followed by gradual destruction of these cells related with growth, after they have reached up to the maximum limit. Complete process of destruction of biological cells gives rise to death of persons. Science can define well about the premature deaths or sudden deaths which are due to biological malfunctioning of cells and goes medically incurable. Intentional and accidental deaths are very painful which are untimed and due to wrongful act of other person responsible for death. But the loss of life has already been done and it cannot be equated in terms of money or punishment.

What I wish to bring before you is that there exists a life even after your death. It could only be perceived through sensibilities of the people you left behind. You are not there to see that what happens after your death, but your great deeds are certainly going to be seen by others, to be experienced by others and off course, people would be benefitted also by all that you did when you lived in this world. You will live now in the hearts of the people. Your greatness would be remembered for all the times in good sense and not your misdeeds. Now it is up to you that you make a determination even to live after your death. Nobody on this earth can stop you from doing good deeds. Do not let anyone to disturb you against your will. Life is very short and you have a long way to go untiring. People die but the world never comes to know about it. When death comes to you, let the people know that you have left this world. You live even after your death.

*"Death never discriminates among individuals, whether rich or poor, big or small. Let us leave a legacy behind so that the world would remember after death. You are not there to see that what happens after your death, but your great deeds are certainly going to be seen by others, to be experienced by others and off course people would be benefitted also by all that you did when you lived in this world. You will live now in the hearts of the people. That should be the purpose of our life objectivity."*

---

# 40

## LISTEN TO INNER VOICE

Whether you notice it or not, there is an unseen vast world inside you in the form of your inner conscience. This world has its own honest observations about human conduct. It speaks also when it finds that any particular human conduct is against to its internal norms. Not only it speaks but it gives directives to stop doing wrongs and warnings also in case wrongs are repeated. But we ignore directives and we do deliberately those acts or omissions which our inner conscience never permits. We keep doing things against the voice of our inner conscience. We also consciously know the acts, to be not in conformity with our inner voice. Ultimately consequences of such acts are bound to be wrongful. We do not even feel repentant for our acts. Now the big question going to be as to who will face the consequences of our own wrongful acts? We only and none else...!!! What does this show? My humble submission is that such deliberate ignorance is going to be very damaging for us in our life. Please listen to your inner voice, do not ignore it.

Your inner conscience always keeps managing about you and about your welfare. No doubt, everybody's life is full of problems. There are problems in your life which you would have to manage with. You might have very cautiously experienced that whenever you happen to face problems your inner conscience always suggests you the most honest and viable solutions for you. Now it is up to you whether you promptly respond to your inner voice. You responded to your inner voice the same moment and found that your problem was solved that easily which you never imagined. On number of occasions we experience that when we know, we are going to do some wrongful act, our inner voice resists for it. It was telling us that we should not do such acts. Have you ever experienced that you are sweating full with your heart beat bumping out? Because you are suppressing your inner voice so you are fighting with internal pressure, resulting in your sweating profusely with increased rates of heart beats. You did an act which your inner conscience did not like and did not permit you to do. Suppression of your inner voice becomes a habit for you, so is the internal pressure you keep developing inside your body system. You must not be surprised that you become heart patient one day with never to recover again and falling slave to medicines. I must submit that you should take it as a resulting warning signal for not listening to your inner voice and going against it.

Kindly think over my humble submissions. Can you survive and live healthy by displeasing your inner conscience? You cannot. Your life management requires a balanced body system management with regard to your daily acts or omissions. If your acts fail to respond positively to your body or mind signals then it adversely affects you. If continued then on long run it develops into health hazards for you. Your mental health is more significant and depends much upon your sound physical health. By ignoring your inner voice one day you are going to make yourself mentally sick. That would be the result of your guilty conscience. Be sure your mental sickness is going to deteriorate your physical health gradually and gradually. Medication is not going to be any remedy then. Now you will reach to a point of no return even if you happen to realize your mistakes. You would not be in a position to repent even. Your inner world gave you enough chances to repent and correct yourself. But you never responded to it. You see, that by the time you realize that it is now too late. Always listen to your inner voice and make your life full with pleasure, peace and happiness.

*"Because you are suppressing your inner voice so you are fighting with internal pressure resulting in your sweating profusely with increased rates of heart beats. You did an act which your inner conscience did not like and did not permit you to do. You must not be surprised that you become a heart patient one day with never to recover again falling slave to medicines."*

---

# 41

## MASTER YOUR THOUGHTS

Your thoughts regulate your behavior in society. Visit to great and rich literatures they are full of valuable thoughts, given by great thinkers of all the times. While reading through these thoughts you would have experienced the kind of psychological strength inside you and freshness with ideas throughout the day. You will also experience a stage that your mind either is full of thoughts or with no thoughts. Mind without thoughts is considered to be a 'zero' state of mind. Attaining 'zero' state at the same time, your mind with full of thoughts should be the ultimate goal of your life. Yes…!!! It is possible. Your mind is full of thoughts but still void. Yes…!!! You can attain 'zero' state of mind once you have established mastery over your thoughts. Your thoughtful mind is your strength but it could be your weakness as well at the same time. It is going to be your strength provided the kind of thoughts you are allowing to enter into your mind, are full with vigor and positive energy to nourish to your mental faculty.

You are the master of your thoughts in the sense that it is for you to decide whether your mind, be with good thoughts or bad thoughts. You need to develop mastery within to control and regulate the thinking patterns of your mind. You should be able to pick and choose such thoughts which give soothing effect to your mind.

Proper nourishment of your mind cells with good nutritive thoughts is very essential for their healthy growth and sustenance. People around you, could be with bad ideas and negative thoughts. You cannot avoid them but you need to be quite alert from them, once you have identified them. While interacting with negative people there are every possibility that they are able to spoil your mind with their negative thoughts. You are not in the habit of keeping negative thoughts in your mind, so you get disturbed. Now it takes a lot of time for you, to clean your mind from such bad thoughts. Your valuable time is also wasted while counteracting with spoiling thoughts. The negative thoughts not only disturb your focused mind but major behavioral changes are also observed in your personality due to the impact of bad thoughts. You look to be quite tense. You are seen unnecessarily shouting at your family members while you return home from your place of work. Your entire family peace is also disturbed. This is not fair. Why others go successful in disturbing your peace of mind? May be they are doing so intentionally to tease you and keep disturbing you. This is going to be testing time for you. Be master of your thoughts and foil their bids to spoil your mind.

It gives me confidence to repeat again that you master your mind. You are the regulator of your mental faculty. Do not allow entry of bad thoughts in your mind. People will not be succeeding to disturb you unless you so allow them to be, to enter your mind. In public social life you cannot avoid such situations but you can regulate yourself instead. Develop yourself mentally so prepared that even if you are sitting amidst full of negativity around but still you remain completely unaffected by it. Value your existence since you have to perform lot of tasks relating to human welfare in your life. Make your mind full with constructive and positive ideas serving welfare of needy people on this earth. Leave no space behind for bad thoughts. Your thoughtful mind reflects in your personality and the kind of confidence which one can read through your body language. With a regular practice of allowing entry of good thoughts, one day your mind will develop resistance power against bad thoughts around and will become immune from them. Be determined then and keep moving ahead. None can disturb you.

*"You need to develop mastery within, to control and regulate the thinking patterns of your mind. Be the master of your mind so that you are able to regulate continuous flow of positivity. You should be able to pick and choose such thoughts which give soothing effect to you mind. Proper nourishment of your mind cells with good nutritive thoughts is very essential for their healthy growth and sustenance. Your thoughtful mind reflects in your personality and body language."*

---

# 42

## DISCIPLINE DAILY PURSUITS

There is a great old saying 'early to bed and early to rise'. But when we observe our daily pursuits it is found that we fail to follow this discipline much knowingly. It is considered that between 9 pm to 10 pm is the best time for us to go to sleep and by 5 am to 6 am is the best time to get up in the morning. By scientific parameters of human body system 8 hours sleep for everyone, is considered to be ideal so that people get up fresh in the morning and remain so throughout the day. Take complete sleep in the night and then feel your body and mind freshness and the work performance throughout the day. You would be surprised to see that your working capacity has been almost doubled. You are getting the results the way you wanted. Disciplined pursuits are very essential in anybody's life. You can very easily observe the impacts of your derailed life management without discipline. You will suffer physical and mental health adversely. As a result you will find loss in your business or in whatever profession you are. Discipline cannot be imposed, it can be just advised. Discipline is good for you, this you need to feel realize and work upon it sincerely.

In the present era of internet communications and cyber regime it becomes very painful to watch that life management of our young generations has completely shattered. No discipline for their own life has been left behind. No disciplined hours for sleep management.

Most of the time they are seen browsing their gadgets, let this be day or nights. As if no internet, no life. I am not talking about professionals who are completely dependent upon internet for their overseas business. They are professional in managing their sleep properly otherwise they understand that they shall not be able to work next day. Digitalization has become the demand of the hour. In global economic environment they need to work day and night shift for the sake of their business schedules.

Our more concern should be for those young generations who are busy with their smart phones and wasting their time and health. The so called social media could have been better utilized as a platform for constructive ideas for social strengthening but it is painful to say that instead it is being openly misused for spreading rumors and fake news with malice for weakening social foundations. It is an act of absolute indiscipline being noticed in recent times. Not only youngsters but elders even are seen chatting on social cites beyond midnight hours. They go to bed with badly tired mind and keep lying in their beds struggling for sleep only to get up by 10 am-11am the next morning. They feel tired for the whole day affecting their work performance. What the kind of this discipline is going to be for them, in managing their life and achieving their pursuits? Our youth need to be properly disciplined today otherwise it is going to damage our social interests. Their metabolic and physiological condition of the body and mind is getting ruined.

Your body metabolism requires that you should have your dinner by 8 pm or before and go to sleep by 9 pm to10 pm. But you are postponing your dinner and getting in the habit of taking it around or even after midnight. Your digestive mechanism is going to be disturbed. What would happen to your breakfast then? It is possibly going to be around noon, the next day. You have completely spoiled the natural metabolism of your body by indiscipline of your daily pursuits. It is warning to you that this way you are in the process of inviting health troubles for yourself. This is completely against the nature. Your body and mind are going to revolt against you one day. By the time it is going to be too late for you. You would not be in a position to repent even. Remember that there are no second innings of your life.

*"Take complete sleep in night you will feel the freshness and find that your working potential has been doubled. Derailed life management without discipline is going to be very harmful to you. You will suffer physical and mental health adversely. As a result you will find loss in your business or in whatever profession you are. Remember that there are no second innings of your life."*

---

# 43

## YOUR PERSONAL EXCELLENCE

Your excellence in life is going to be quite personal for you. It would be personal in the sense that you are going to achieve it by your honest and personal sincere efforts. There could be great people who can support you in your pursuit for excellence but it is always your personal effort which would be determining factor in scaling the height of glory in the sky. Your untiring efforts for years altogether would be guarantee for your excellence. Always try to be world class. Never compromise with your achievements less than world class. It is not this world which is going to give you any certificate of excellence but it is your inner world only which would keep on encouraging you and put you on top of this world. You might have noticed that in this world whenever you achieve in your life, your parents are the happiest persons on this earth. Your personal excellence is always directly proportional to their happiness. Always keep this fact in your mind and make them happy. When you are happy then you will sprinkle happiness among the people all around you.

How are you going to be excellent? Make sure that this is not going to happen overnight. You would have to pass through innumerable sleepless nights in pursuit of your excellence. Your pursuit for excellence needs action on your part honestly and sincerely. You have to be very selective in your actions which suit to your capability and temperament. Some times out of over enthusiasm you happen to take up actions beyond your capabilities and you suffer setbacks. These setbacks would induce in you frustration and disappointment. But it is your inner willpower which keeps on encouraging you that you have to excel. You are suffering setbacks do not mean that your actions are gone wasted. You fell into adversities for which you were not prepared. In life you never know the kind of adversities you are going to face across. But one thing is certain that these rigors of your life are going to make you shine much brighter towards the path of you excellence. Many succumb to the onslaughts of failures and become forgotten lots. Those who muster the courage to face the onslaughts they survive and excel ultimately.

In whatever fields of knowledge you are, the excellence refers to one who is on the top of the world. You are a devoted researcher whether scientific or social, taking extra pain which segregates you from others. This is possible, only when you discover a branch of knowledge which was till then unheard of. In case you are an advocate, you practice the knowledge of law so honestly and intelligently that even judges listen to your arguments with due respect. This reflects your excellence by virtue of the kind of credibility you possess that you are no way going to compromise with your excellence or to cheat the law officers. You command an image in the eyes of the administrators of the legal system that you are a staunch believer in the rule of law. You never go for an argument in your files which may defraud them, they know it. That's the kind of excellence you have earned by practicing upon you for decades altogether that you do not make money through malpractices. However, it would have been much easy task for you to mint money, had you been for money making. This is quite personal to you but this thought process did not happen to you overnight. You remember those early days of your career when you struggled through sleepless nights but you never surrendered to any setback. Now when you look back you find that those all troubles were good. Always remember that facing failures in life with never to give up attitude, paves your way for par excellence. You could know then that you were born to excel.

*"Never compromise with your achievements less than world class. Your pursuit for excellence needs action on your part honestly and sincerely. You are suffering setbacks it does not mean that your efforts are wasted. Many succumb to the onslaughts of failures and become forgotten lots. Those who muster the courage to face the onslaughts they survive and excel ultimately."*

———————————————————

# 44

## THE PEOPLE YOU ASSOCIATE

The company you keep, highly matters. There is an important saying that you are going to be known, like the kind of people you are associating with. Exceptions are always there. It is found to be very rare that people remain unaffected despite amidst bad people. But this is not possible for everyone. People with certain characters, like and prefer to live in company of people with similar characters. Social behaviors are learnt while living in the society. This learning is by way of imitation and follow ups. A person imitates certain behaviors of other persons because of his living in their company. Such kind of imitations is quite inherent in human behavior. One would learn and imitate good habits if he associates with good people. A person who is living in company of bad people he will imitate bad habits by virtue of his bad association. The process starts in a person right from his childhood. The learning process in such associations is developed through intimate groups of various kinds depending upon frequency and time intervals they use to pass in each other's company.

We need to understand the human psychology behind such associations. Sociology makes it categorically clear that man is a social animal. Since he has to live in this society and has to maintain social relationships then he is dependent upon people in society. Social obligations are based upon social interactions so one cannot keep aloof from society. That's right. But at the same time he has to be selective enough in choosing company of the people. The human associations are carried upon with the level of understanding amongst its members. Intellectual associations could be seen based on the similar levels. At the same time there are common people too who are innocent and pure by their heart. Every human being is fair by nature. They intend to live with feelings of mutual co-existence, so they associate. But human history is much with conspiracies too. Such conspiracies are as a state of human mind where two or more persons come to an agreement to cause harm to some other person. This is a complete negative orientation part of human mind and conspiracy in the sense that such persons have a malicious intention to cause harm to others in society who intend for mutual relationships with good intentions. My point of discussion here is that you have to be always careful and protect yourself from such negatively oriented minds. The only safe way to do that is to keep you at a distance from such people. Do not associate or live in company of such people whom you consider to be not good for social interests.

The weaker element of people's psychology is that they always prefer simple and easy roads to move on, rather than to encounter with difficulties. Company of average people looks to be quite easy and pleasant that is why people get attracted to such associations. Cheap things look quite easy to be enjoyed with since they are very easily available. But always keep this fact in mind that such pleasures of average level are going to take you nowhere. Keeping in company of honest and value minded people would be very difficult for those who are not honest and devoid of values. Your company matters because you will be known by the company of the people you have. So associating in the company of highest level will be of much benefit to you in the sense that your thinking pattern and mindset would also be of the highest order. Always have preferential aptitude right from the early days of your life with relation to the group of persons you are associating with. A single mistake in selecting good people is going to harm you in due course of your life particularly when you wish to be a man of highest order while you live in this world.

*"Keeping in company of honest and value minded people would be very difficult for those who are not honest and devoid of values. A person who is living in company of bad people he will imitate bad habits by virtue of his bad association. Your company matters because you will be known by the company of people you have. Be selective while choosing good people of the highest order."*

---

# 45

## READING GREAT BOOKS

Develop habit of reading great thought provoking books. You will be very easily able to get this habit if you are selective in picking up rich literature. Your peaceful mind demands nutritious thoughts and the books rich with positivity provide the needed nutrition to your mind. Try to find out the truth behind the great old saying that 'books have proved to be men's best friends'. You need to have a good library with you full of books with nice and rich ideas. While sitting in your library in conversation with your books, you will never feel lonely. Those who do not have reading habits, it becomes very difficult for them to pass their time. It may sound strange that books converse. Try to get any such occasion to watch people who are in conversation with books and exchanging thoughts. The most revealing feature of books is that take them for granted on their face value. They have nothing to conceal provided you get in touch with good books. The books which are on development of human civilizations, revealing history of great nations, the notable discoveries on this earth, motivational struggles made by the great people, adventurous stories, the philosophies of great thinkers all across the globe, top categories books on science and technological research which express their concern for benefit of the mankind. You will find great thoughts for establishing social justice, economic and educational justice for the vast areas of human interest which need to be learnt time and again by our generations. Doing what is just and fair for not only human beings but for the whole universe could best be understood from relevant books on the subject. Literature on protection of human rights has proved to be of basic concern in present era.

Mental exercise is very essential for sharpness of the human brain. Books are the only tools for such mental exercise. Reading through books particularly with thought provoking ideas give you a fertile ground to generate your own view points to address with. Where you have made books to be your good friends they are going to prove to be your best friends. Books are never going to disappoint you subject to the fact that the nature and qualities of books you are looking for. Our markets are full with below quality books to satisfy the taste of such readers who search for it to please their senses. Appeasing sexually colored tastes are much in number. The publishers with cheap content orientations come out with such category of books to make money. Such is the kind of literature which is going to permanently spoil the human mind. Such low level books may give momentary sensual pleasure to individuals but the kind of damaging lust they are going to infuse in human minds is disappointing. State law regulating agencies fail to come out with any effective punitive measures to stop such low level books to be sold in the markets. Once our generations are in the tight grips of human lust it gets to be very difficult to bring them out of it. We seriously need to liberate our generations from such below level books and divert their attention through good thought provoking books. Good books are live assets for us. It becomes our liability to preserve them nicely for the benefit of our future generations.

Identifying good books is no big problem. First of all you need to develop a kind of reading habit. Your areas of interest could be very varied. The books which are going to motivate you and ignite within you a kind of positive action are best. Such books which make you feel to be mentally strong full with thought provoking spirits should be your choice. Negativity in one's mind is more dominating in comparison to positivity. We need to make conscious efforts to kill negativity within us and keep improving upon positivity. Such efforts would only be possible when we are going to make it a daily habit of reading great books.

*"Your peaceful mind demands nutritious thoughts. It may sound strange, but books converse. The most revealing feature of books is that take them for granted on their face value. They have nothing to conceal. Good books are live assets for us. It becomes our liability to preserve them nicely for the benefit of our future generations."*

---

# 46

## BE PATIENT LISTENER

People look quite impatient while they keep on talking themselves instead of listening to others. They want to keep talking and expecting others to listen to them. They could also be seen imposing their ideas over others. They would have to see that whether the other people are ready to listen to or accept their ideas or not. If the other person goes on talking like that while the other people are paying no attention to his talks then his whole effort proves to be a futile exercise. There is famous saying that 'be a patient listener'. Let us examine this saying in its true letters and spirit. Instead of getting talkative one should be a patient listener too. This is considered to be great quality. We often find it very rare such people who listen to other's talks with a concentrated mind. Listening patiently means concentrating to what others say. Patience affords an opportunity not only listening to but simultaneously understanding the qualitative contents of the talk and later applying such contents for welfare of people at large. It is seen that we do not find us properly concentrating to the other's talk because the other person does not happen to be a good orator. More often we find speeches to be quite boring so we start losing our patience. How to make a speech to be interesting is an art? No doubt about it that good orators attract good audience but it never means that the speakers who are not good orators are devoid of quality contents in their speeches. Thus if we wish to be benefitted by the contents of the speech we have to be patient and concentrating on. You will find that the good orators develop a kind of expertise with the passage of time and are able to bind the audience by their fluent oratory. But that is altogether a different situation.

Being a patient listener is a good character of human conduct. A patient audience not only motivates the speaker to speak on with much informative knowledge but you can watch the communication capacity also comes out with full confidence. Moreover, you also as a speaker expect to be a good and patient audience when it is your turn to speak. You need to concentrate more on the contents of other's speech rather than his oratory. Information is comparatively more important to your patient listener because on the subject person is speaking he has worked a lot and has collected valuable material to share with the audience and you are among the audience or may be sharing with him on the dais. Do not claim yourself to be perfect with knowledge. This tendency of feeling to be perfect with knowledge hampers your ability to learn more and proves damaging to pursuit of knowledge in the long run. The psychological thinking that one is perfect with knowledge makes one impatient while listening to others. Such mentality is going to cause harm in search for knowledge. You have to concentrate on subjective and material part of even a boring lecture. It will benefit you since you acquired more knowledge in its material particulars.

This universe is abundant with knowledge. You have to keep learning and learning lifelong. This is only possible when you develop yourself to be a patient listener when you happen to be in any conference, meeting or interactive group discussions. It is agreed that all talks may not be up to the quality. Don't be there where unnecessary argumentative talks are going on. Not only you would be wasting your time in such low quality talks but there would be negative bearing also to your thinking process. It is not advisable to be the part of such gatherings where talk standards is below the level. Being a patient listener is going to help you in the sense that you will be able to equip yourself with varied kind of knowledge and its delivery afterwards with confidence.

*"Be a patient listener. You need to concentrate more on the contents of other's speech rather than his oratory. Information is more important to your patient listener. Do not claim yourself to be perfect with knowledge. This attitude would damage your capacity to learn more. Do not be part of a talk which is below level. This universe is abundant with knowledge. Acquire that with all patience."*

---

# 47

## POSITIVE CHANGING

Time is ever changing. This world is ever changing. I fail to understand sometimes whether time in fact is changing? How come time is going to change? It is always moving constantly with set geographical patterns. Seasonal variations are quite obvious but that too constant with climatic cycles. Man made changes apart; this world is also not changing. In fact the truth is that, we as a human being are changing. Sometimes we change positively while on other times we change negatively. The frequency, with which we change negatively, is much on the higher side then our positive changes. Such changing is not the problem of time. That is our problem created by us. We in actual sense are the real problem makers and are responsible to disturb the entire geographical system making them into changing frames.

Nature is always positive for us. The natural resources are abundant with life and space. We are unfortunate to explore the life and peace in the nature. We have indiscriminately ruined the balance of nature. This is an extreme negative mindset of a man. Nature has already started showering its destructive impact on this earth. The world is witnessing the most devastating pandemic of the century in the form of outbreak of novel corona virus Covid-19 which has already claimed more than 3,74,400 human lives where more than 62,95,500 population already infected all across the globe with this corona virus by 01st of June, 2020. The most burning questions before us today are whether the stage we have reached? Who is going to save us from our own negativities? Whether we have already reached to a point of no return? Damage has already been done to the nature. Nature knows better that how it should balance itself. We are just witnessing helplessly frightened with, the balancing patterns of nature, closed from behind the locked down world, as silent spectators. We have put our generations in the grip of danger. Nature has always been generous for us looking to our past deeds but it struck only when we crossed the limits. We are now in urgent need for taking serious remedial steps towards damage control before it is too late. We feel that if it would be a point of no return but still there must be a ray of hope provided this world comes out with positive changes. It would then otherwise prove to be the last and final call for humanity.

What could be the remedy then? It is not only that we play with the nature but we similarly behave negative towards our fellow human beings. Discrimination among fellow human beings is absolutely unnatural but still we do. The world faces the consequences of its own kind. Why there is poverty on this earth? Not only poverty, there are people who are living below the poverty line. Where are the managers of world system? Are they actually helpless to eradicate poverty on this earth? Or they maliciously doing nothing and letting people die of hunger and malnutrition. Don't you come across the reporting of starvation deaths? Did you notice the fate of migrant labor in India during corona crisis? They are seen dying painfully on railway tracks, road sides, on board trains, of hunger due to defective state policies. Who is to be made accountable for such system failures? Who is bothered even for introducing positive changes? None else…!!! Elected governments are feeling comfortable in their own political business in making governments and unmaking oppositions. Welfare orientations of common and needy men have been completely lost. Humanity cannot be served with properly, unless positive changing in the socio-economic and political scenario is introduced with humanitarian considerations. This is only possible when our governments are more human than political. They should muster the courage to lose their governments for the sake of positive changing.

*"Nature is always positive for us. Natural resources are abundant with life and space. We are unfortunate to explore the life and peace in the nature. We have indiscriminately ruined the balance of nature. Discrimination among fellow human beings is unnatural too. The world today needs positive changes. We need governments more human than political."*

---

# 48

## DRAW THE FRAMEWORK

While you plan for your successful life, always draw a framework so that you can write something on it prospectively. Make a frame and paint your life beautifully in it. Painting your life on the framework is the vision for your life. Every one of us should have a life vision to make our life beautiful. Try to see the colours of life on it and feel the kind of hidden pleasures of life. We have got human life so it is for us to look for all possible situations to make it more peaceful and pleasant. It is in our hands to draw the framework of life. The painted picture would not only depict your present but it will also very nicely reflect the great possibilities of your future. Your life frame would also define the conduct rules of your life management. You will take a pledge that you will strictly abide with your rules for life. You will not go beyond the framework so drawn by you. Without making any framework for your life you will always be violating your own rules and norms set by you. Life management is very important for everyone otherwise your life will move haphazardly in any direction getting out of your control. It is your life so it must be well within your control. Nobody wants chaos in his life. Chaos means nothing is happening in your life the way you wish for. All appears to be not well. You find that thing are going to be out of order. Life without order is nothing but disappointment. This breeds frustration in you hampering the progress of your life

Doing in conformity with your directives so framed by you would be quite interesting. Making your life framework and then violating it would be damaging. Keep this virtual fact in mind that your framework is going to make you lead a well disciplined life. And you best understand the value of discipline in your life. You need to work for your life frame considering as if, it is the Constitution of your life. It will be the life's vision document. You honestly understand that if you happen to violate the terms and conditions of your life's Constitution then you deserve to be punished. Who will punish you then? You need to make a provision for self-punishment in case you acted in a manner in your life, amounting to violation of the rules in your framework. Since the life rules in your framework are self prepared, you will be under moral obligation bound to follow your life rules. No other person is going to punish you for breach of self made rules. You would have no reasons to blame any other person that rules were imposed upon you against your will which you find difficult to follow on. You best understand your capacity to work, so frame the life rules accordingly. To my understanding life moral rules are to be framed and followed. They are not based subject to your capacity but they are essential to induce moral strength inputs in your life framework.

Drawing framework are well defined routes for your success and following them scrupulously is the secret of your smooth life management. How you have to behave and when you have to restrict yourself? When you are drawing the framework for your life, you have to self-discipline yourself that you are not going to exceed the limits framed by you only. If you are honest enough then any violation by you will make you feel guilty with a conviction not to repeat again. It is understood that phases of struggles are tough. It goes sometimes beyond the capacities of human behaviour to strictly keep content himself within the framework drawn. That's fine but it cannot be accepted as any logic to justify your breach of code of conduct. Frame your life management rules to honestly follow. Let the Almighty bless you the strength.

*"Try to see the colours of life in your framework and feel the kind of hidden pleasures of your life. Let your framework be the Constitution of your life. Self made rules would inculcate in you the moral strength and the much needed sense of self discipline. Your life rules should not be capacity based but they should be moral obligations for you. It will be the life's vision document putting you under moral obligation to scrupulously follow it in your life management. You make provisions for self punishment in case you happen to violate self made rules."*

---

# 49

## MISSION OF YOUR LIFE

You are born on this earth with a mission. Obviously looking to your level of thinking your life mission must be world class. It is not sufficient to make a mission but equally significant would be that you should not feel repenting in the fag end of your life that you could not achieve your life mission. The biggest life mission everyone has that he should do deeds in his life so that at the time of his death the man should die with peace in his mind. To live with peace is in consonance with to die with peace. Welfare begets a sense of welfare. Positivity begets a sense of positivity. It is very simple that your life mission should be like that it never makes you feel to be full with guilty conscious at any point of time in your life. Make sure this way you have very happily achieved your mission of life. If you fail to accomplish the mission of your life then it is proved to be complete waste. When you did for your mission you lived your life forever. Every person, who is born, has to die one day. But with your mission accomplished, you will die your celebrated death which would be remembered in the years to come. Have you ever thought as to what should be the mission of your life? Or you are just dragging your life without any mission? You think once.

Your life's mission would be the 'end' of your life. If you are living your life with thinking in your mind, as if every day is going to be the last day of your life, make sure you cannot commit wrongful acts even in your distant dreams. It is common human psychology that a man fears death. At the same time he has also witnessed many deaths to be quite painful. Who will not like to avoid a painful death? Why can't it be the mission of your life? Your mission is going to be the 'end' of your life, so you need to develop 'means' to achieve the 'end' of your life. Making the 'end' and developing the 'means' accordingly is exclusively your area. It may take whole life time for you in developing the 'means' while you reach to the 'end' of your life. Even if you happen to develop the 'means' well in advance, you need to serve the 'mission' of your life till you reach the 'end' of your life, provided you wish to die with peace for sure. Every person has the wish to die a peaceful death and the people are fortunate who die peacefully. Not everyone would have a peaceful death. Accomplishing peace of mind should be the ultimate mission of your life. You look for such means which give you peace of mind and happiness. Once you have attained this stage, rest assure you have won over the death. It could be one of the situations when one happens to lead saintly life. But you are in worldly life and then making your life lead as saintly life.

It is possible living worldly life and at the same time keeping content with peace of mind. Always prefer to do such acts for others which are going to get you a feel of pleasure. This could be absolutely your choice to choose an area of your likings and convenience. You may be having your own limitations. No problem. You can make some space honestly to help those who are genuinely in need of your help. Be honest to the extent that you don't expect taking back the help you rendered to them. Giving graciously and then forgetting about it gives a kind of immense pleasure which is unparallel of any worldly gains. You may be having your own family liabilities, hardships in your life, moments of more pains less pleasure. These are going to be testing times for you in true sense, while ignoring your pains you are coming out to help others. You are standing in support and helping others probably you have discovered those 'means' to achieve the 'end' of your life.

*"To live with peace is in consonance with to die with peace. The biggest life mission everyone has that he should do deeds in his life so that at the time of his death, the man should die with peace in his mind. Giving graciously and then forgetting about it gives a kind of immense pleasure which is unparallel of any worldly gains. You come out helping others while ignoring your pains. Thus making your life's missions complete. Your mission is the 'end' and the tools are the 'means' to achieve the 'end' of life. You achieve the 'means' and the 'end' of your life too."*

# 50

## LIFE IS PLEASANT STORY

Make life a pleasant story for others. Life is not going to be the same again. Enjoy your present today, since it is running fast and is going to be your past very soon. Never say like others that who has seen the future? You can very well see your future based upon your actions you are performing today. No doubt, your past has been gone and you are supposed to live in present. Your life becomes a pleasant story for others when you leave this world. Your humanitarian acts for others make it to be more pleasant. Where everybody thinks for himself and for protecting interests of his relatives, you are thinking for the welfare of the others and doing it also whenever possible. That is going to be your greatness. Your life is a pleasant story for you also. Think about your life and its beauty. Feel gratuitous towards your life. Your life has given you a lot of happiness in the form of your achievements. Never complain. Sufferings in your life are an integral part of it. But your efforts must be to keep looking for those fewer moments of joy which make your life a beautiful journey. Your life journey should maintain the beauty of your life. Have you ever been able to witness the kind of beauty, your life has? You will only be able to realize this beauty of your life, when you are going to develop a support system within you, not only to maintain but keep enhancing this life beauty as well. Take out at least thirty minutes daily from your busy schedule either in the morning or in the evening hours, whenever it suits to you. Sit alone with focused mind and your eyes closed thinking about yourself. Feel that you attained the void of your mind. Your mind has gone completely empty with no thoughts. Experience the happiness waves spreading across your body and the sensation of the joy around. Pleasant story of your life begins the moment you have taken the determination that you will not think bad for others. You will completely ignore if anybody thinks bad for you. This habit is going to give you such a relief from within, which you would have never imagined.

May be you are a believer in God, you may not be even. It hardly matters for anybody. There is no second opinion that there is an invisible force which controls and regulates the entire universe. You connect yourself with that force. That would be enough for the pleasant story to feel realize. These thirty minutes in isolation would be significant for you. Try to search yourself and roam around your serene mind. You feel the rhythm of your heart beats. The sensation which you are experiencing, you enjoy your journey that you are so close to your life beats. You are romancing with your life and the heart beats are making you still romantic.

During thirty minutes daily be in conversation with you. Talk to your life and share your feelings with it that you are so obliged to get an opportunity to live with cheers. Your daily actions are going to determine that you had a nice meeting with your life. Review what you did yesterday? Share your review with your life. Your life is the best mentor for you watching your actions very carefully and keeps suggesting measures in case you fell in any trouble. Very honestly and transparently if you find that you did something against the life measures and which your conscious did not allow, then determine to never repeat it again. Such life reviews are going to establish a happy bonding with your life. Plan for the day which you are going to perform and accomplish. Every day the pleasant story of your life starts with your day. Night is the rest time so that you continue with afresh the next day to add more joy with ongoing life story.

*"Your life becomes pleasant story for others when you leave this world. Take out thirty minutes daily from your busy schedule and think about you with your eyes closed. Try to search yourself and roam around your serene mind. You feel the rhythm of your heart beats. The sensation which you are experiencing, you enjoy your journey that you are so close to your life beats. You are romancing with your life and the heart beats are making you still romantic."*

---

# 51

## LIVING THE LAST DAY

This is a very great thinking that you live your life as if you are living the last day of your life. You have got the life not just to waste it away but achieve something substantial, so that future generations remember you for your deeds. Life is not certain but death is certain then why to fear death? Who knows? Today one is living with all his occupations and tomorrow he is no more. He was not able to see the light of the day. He and his relatives never knew that today was his last day. Understanding the philosophy of life and death is very simple. There is no need to search for any mystery behind it. It's like a bubble which vanishes any moment. The moment life ceases to exist in living organisms the life sciences experts proclaim it death. Live it up to your life today for good deeds; no one knows what is going to happen tomorrow. Make death feel your strength in the sense that this would stop you from being negligent, unjust and arbitrary. It would inculcate in you the kind of orientation to be honest and to humane towards others for the reasons that the death of human life is the last eternal truth.

It is a common human psychology that no one wants to die. Obviously, when life is so beautiful then everyone wants to enjoy this life. But all in the society are not so fortunate that life is beautiful for them. They are born in scarcities, live in and die too in scarcities.

They also enjoy their life own way. Enjoying life is a feeling, though scarcity matters but it cannot stop people from feeling full with joy. Despite abundance people are not able to enjoy life as if they die every day. Connect yourself with those people who are suffering from chronic diseases. Doctors attending to their treatment are absolutely hopeless to save their life. They understand the disease to be incurable as per their knowledge about medical sciences. Doctors have given the final word to their attendants. All are sitting full with grief and waiting for the death to arrive at. May be the patient under treatment has no knowledge about the bitter truth that the death is waiting in front of him. He has not been informed about it as a matter of precaution under rules. But the person on the death bed is more conscious about what is happening around? He could read the message writ large on the faces of his nearer and dearer. Though they never communicated to him about his ensuing death which was imminent but they could not conceal the truth either. Their body language was more communicative. They were helpless. The person in the meantime mentally prepared himself to depart from this world.

Try to reach up to the psychology of the man who is visibly watching the death standing in front of him. May be today, could be his last day on this earth. It could be even few days more. All the good deeds and bad deeds done by him in the past are moving like a running movie before his eyes. He repents to his bad deeds done. Starts weeping out vigorously and begging from the death that can't he be spared for some more days? He wanted do some more good deeds worth living and seek excuses for his bad deeds. He begs for to die with peace. But the last truth of human life prevails. Let us not forget that nature has much strict laws to be adhered to by us. But we ignore them mercilessly. The man made system on earth may discriminate but death never discriminates and implements its rule very strictly and scrupulously. You did bad deeds; you deliberately ignored the rules of nature. Now when on death bed you are begging for your life to be spared once. No way. Death is certain. Try to live your life as if you are living the last day of your life by doing good deeds for others so that you die in peace without any feeling of remorse.

*"Understanding the philosophy of life and death is very simple. The moment life ceases to exist in living organisms the life sciences experts proclaim it death. Live it up to your life today for good deeds; no one knows what is going to happen tomorrow. Make death feel your strength in the sense that this would stop you from being negligent, unjust and arbitrary. Live your life with this conviction that as if you are living today as last day of your life."*

---

# 52

## THINK UNIQUE WAY

It is the thinking of a person which makes him either good or bad. Your pattern of thinking matters since it gives an idea about your mind. A man would behave in positive manner provided his thinking patterns are positive. A man behaving so as to causing harm to others is indicative of his negative patterns of thinking. Whatever you think it is always reflected in your body language. You cannot conceal the reflections of your ideas into your behavior. Firstly your thinking is going to affect you, your personality and the gathering around you. Your thinking also makes its own impact on your decision making and its subsequent execution on different occasions. There are people who are strict decision makers since they think honest and without any prejudice. They mean business that is why they are strict decision makers. You can see in them that they are transparent in their administration and never like to cut a sorry figure. I have talked about the thinking patterns to be positive or negative. One thing comes to my mind that can we afford to be thinking neutral or for that matter to be 'thinking unique' way? Yes…!!! That is possible.

What amounts to be 'thinking unique' need to be given a serious thought? True, this would be a big exercise and difficult task. You are a unique personality. You don't think the way others think. You think differently and you have your own logic to show the way you think.

No doubt in your thinking 'unique way' positive orientation of your mind has its dominating share. May be there are majority of people who believe that God exists but you may be unique in the sense that you do not believe in the existence of God. You have unique reasoning for such a belief. You are not a blind follower in searching of the belief whether God exists? You are in the habit of dismissing superstitions because such beliefs give rise to blind faith, without any logic or reason. Governments overlook deliberately but you are perturbed by the prevailing poverty conditions in the society. There are big numbers of poor, sick and hungry people sitting outside the places of worship begging for the food day and night. There physical and mental conditions are not that sound if they should be asked to put in hard labor and earn for themselves. The believers may be waiting for some divine justice to happen someday and things would be automatically upright. You believe in that these are the needy people to whom the God should extend the helping hand. The world witnessed that during Covid-19 pandemic outbreak all the places of worship remained through under lockdown conditions while people died helplessly begging for their life. You think differently that there is no convincing logic for you as to how come divinity is going to help them out of such exceptional situations? Science and technology has its logical and factual analysis to justify number of events. It is no any magic all the way.

What the welfare states have been doing so far? If the governments in systematic political governance are going to be impotent all the way then how come the divine belief would be of any help to eradicate such pandemic conditions? We need to work upon it consciously by taking affirmative action in such directions. Divine belief must be that things should go well in the society. No doubt it could be indicative of one's bonafide intention but that is not all in itself. In a society where working atmosphere has almost gone to the point of absolute carelessness, your thinking in unique way only is going to help you out. It must be an all out dictation for welfare of the mankind.

*"Think neutral for that matter thinking unique having positive orientation of mind with its dominating share. There are big numbers of poor, sick and hungry people sitting outside the places of worship begging for food day and night. The believers may be waiting for some divine justice to happen someday and things would be automatically upright. You think unique way that it's no any magic. You look for the logic if such beliefs perpetuate that way."*

---

# 53

## POTENTIAL MIND

Potential minds are those which have exceptional fertile capacity ready with workable ideas. Sharp minds are very sensitive too. You might have heard about razor sharp minds which cut across ideas very potentially. The strength of such minds has been directly related with the physical soundness of the person. The wavelength equations of potential minds is of such a high quality that on occasions it becomes very difficult for the people of average minds to understand properly. If people with average understanding happen to be in majority and any communication from sharp potential minds, goes much above across their heads and beyond their understanding then without much delay these majority 'average minds' declare the potential 'sharp mind' to be 'insane mind'. This way great loss is caused to the humanity which remains deprived of advantages of potential minds. It is my humble submission that one should never bother for all such damaging acts of average majority minds. They would do only what they are up to. Without getting bothered, you do what you are destined to do towards advancement of human civilizations. Your mind possesses enormous potential. You decide to be successful in your life. This decision has been taken by your mind first. If you happen to think to be a great scientist, any politician or Nobel laureate, this idea first of all comes to your mind. Then you honestly start working upon your plan with a specific mindset and you get the success. Honesty is a state of mind which goes to enrich your mind's potential and makes it sharper. The moment you realize that your mind is not supporting, you start losing your heart. You find that things are not happening the way you wanted them to be.

Have you ever observed the functioning of you mind? The mind is the controlling center of your entire bodily activities. The nature has given equal potential to every human mind. Our world history is full of such warriors who have won the battles on the strength of their mind only. The strategies they made with strict executions and they conquered. Now the question may arise when every mind has equal potential then how come the sharp minds get dominated over others? Yes…!!! That is true. How does a mind get sharp and sharper? Think that you are using your mind much less, may be almost unused. Sharpness of your mind would depend upon the rate of frequency your mind is put to mental exercises. You keep using your mind in solving out such ticklish problems which others usually tend to avoid. Like mathematical exercises are good for your mental sharpness but you would find not much people who do take interest in solving mathematical problems.

Exceptions apart, sharp potential minds are not born, they are made. As we have discussed above that biologically every human mind possesses equal grey matter but it is the regular exercise which keeps enhancing potentiality of the mind. Then why to envy others if they have a sharp mind? We too had equal opportunities to sharp our mind but we didn't. Practicing with mind is a very rigorous exercise through days and nights and years altogether. You will not feel tired when you exercise your mind with a mission which generates enthusiasm. When you are pursuing your mind with a selfless mission then you yourself would feel realize the enormous potential of your mind. You would have to develop the mindset by working upon it regularly. You would find one day that strength of your mind is flowing so smoothly that you are enjoying even the every bit of its potential for a cause you best pursue.

*"Sharp potential minds are very fertile and sensitive too. Think about razor sharp minds. Your mind possesses enormous potential. Biologically every human mind possesses equal grey matter. Sharpness of your mind would depend upon the rate of frequency your mind is put to mental exercises. Like mathematical exercises are good for your mental sharpness but you would find not much people who do take interest in solving mathematical problems."*

# 54

## BEAUTY OF NATURE

The beauty of nature is that it always gives, it never takes from others. The nature has its own laws which it follows scrupulously and it does not discriminate. Have you ever experienced the beauty of nature? It is beautiful and one can say that it is full with beauty. You would have to live with nature if you so wish, making yourself subject to the laws of nature. You are managing your life strictly as per rules of nature then there is no reason that you would not be able to live your life enjoying with beauty of the nature. Whenever there would be a debate whether nature came first or the human life, the conclusion would be go in favor of the nature. Human life on this earth owes its existence to the protective umbrella of nature. The abundant resources of the nature remained at the disposal of we the people so that we can survive with and our coming generations too. The water flows in the rivers, the wind blowing across the mountains standing on the top, while the trees down with fruits, all looks like a fairy tale. How it sounds good that we feel obliged for the nature which has endowed us with its treasures? It is the Mother Nature which is spreading all fragrance of its beauty to its creatures on this earth.

Do we ever feel that we have become so self-centered and do not think to reciprocate with the nature? If not reciprocating then at least no harm caused to the nature. No matter, we don't even deserve to reciprocate with the nature since we have left no effort behind to play foul with the nature. We are going rampant to destroy the nature and spoil its beauty. We have already disturbed the natural balance in the name of indiscriminate development. When we start facing the adversities of such imbalances then we don't have any plausible excuses to put forward to justify our misdeeds, we have done with the nature. We are ruthlessly cutting down trees and destroying our forests. Due to this large scale deforestation, weather patterns have been disturbed as never before. Monsoons are reported to be either running very late or no monsoons. Our rivers are gone without water and rains have become scary. Natural disasters are no more new events for us and have become order of the day. They have become very common causing huge loss of life and property on the earth. Science is absolutely helpless to have developed any device to prevent such catastrophes and save human lives. It can only have indicative signals for predicting such happening as a precautionary measure so that people of such areas could immediately evacuate and taken to safer places. Any distraction in such signals can cause havoc within fraction of minutes.

Let us not seek answers for such perturbing questions as to who is responsible for such unpredictable behavior of nature? First we go on destroying the beauty of nature indiscriminately and then keep debating to protect and conserve it, are all foolish and not excusable. World summits are held on regular intervals to discuss issues relating to degradation of environment. Resolutions so passed during such summits appear to be quite reasonable. The concerns so expressed by the member nations are quite genuine. What is questionable is that they would awake only when they are faced with the problem knocking at the doorsteps? Now they are scared of the mankind balancing on the verge of destruction. Even after such critical situations no serious effort are seen round the corner for honest enforcement of summit resolutions at the grass root levels. Let us all we warned that careless enforcement of summit resolutions are going to further deteriorate situations and beauty of the nature.

*"Nature is beautiful one can say that it is full with beauty. Human life on this earth owes its existence to the protective umbrella of the nature. We are ruthlessly cutting down trees and destroying our forests. Due to this large scale deforestation weather patterns have been disturbed as never before. Monsoons are reported to be either running very late or no monsoons. Our rivers are gone without water and rains have become very scary."*

# 55

# MANAGE YOUR TIME

You can very well understand the significance of time management in your life successes. Time is never static and it always keeps moving. You have to do lot many great works in your short life when you may be feeling that you are running short of time. If you are not a good time manager then it would be a gone case for you. The moment you fail to manage your time it flies away like anything. You will keep running behind it, just in your desperate bid to catch it but all in vain and making you collapse with tears in your eyes. But once time has gone it never comes back. Every person has equal 24 hours in a day at his disposal. The winners manage these hours in a most productive manner and become successful but the losers fail to utilize these hours and waste their entire life. Time management stresses about the need that what you are planning to do tomorrow, do it today itself. And what you plan to do today, do it right now. Who knows what is going to happen in the next moment? You never know. Don't leave anything for tomorrow else, you will prove to be a failure since tomorrow never comes. Time management in life is very important. Time is very precious in the sense that it is running continuously by its nature. It never waits for anybody. No science can evolve any mechanism which may enable people to save time and keep it in their balance accounts as their savings to spend in future. Time capsules are not sold in the markets so that one can purchase the same and utilize for himself whenever he so feels. You need to develop your own self-desire and to save your time by getting very calculative.

For best managing your time there is no time machine which is going to calculate and manage the time for you. It is you only who holds the key to be worried about it, to plan and manage your time. No doubt, it is your life and you better understand the mission you would be looking for. You have to plan your projects by yourself. Some of your projects may be of much time taking. Therefore, you will have to buy time from your lesser projects and fix priorities subject to the conditions of your work performance and its delivery thereafter. You have absolutely no time, to waste in foul talks. Always there are people who may try to take undue advantage of situations and may waste your time and energy unproductively which do not suit to your life objectives. They may keep sitting with you, talking all useless subjects for hours since they are in the habit of wasting time. Such practices are unhealthy for your pursuits. Identify such people right in the beginning and keep at a distance from them. Never allow them to unnecessarily interfere with your daily projects and waste your valuable time.

The primary condition for managing your time is that you should plan your day nicely. Your project may be of long duration but you have to manage your time on daily basis while keep focusing to its finality. Even wastage of one day from your time slot is going to cost you heavily. It is seen that planning is easy but moving according to fixed time schedules and its strict implementation thereafter becomes very difficult. This is due to lack of needed will power. Time management is essential because successful are those who are the best time managers. Within a certain span of your life when you are physically and mentally active, you need to achieve a lot of your life objectives. By the time your life would be passing away, your number of plans would remain pending and you would never find time to work upon them. So move ahead, manage your time if you have a mission of your life and you seriously intend to achieve it.

*"Time is never static and it always keeps moving. Every person has equal 24 hours in a day at his disposal. Winners are able to beautifully manage it while losers fail. Time management in life is very essential. Time is precious in the sense that it is running fast for mismanagement. It never waits for anybody. You have absolutely no time to waste in foul talks. Successful are those who are the best time managers and strict executers."*

---

# 56

## THE BEST YOU

Whatever circumstances are there, the best must come out of you. There may be situations in your life which are not favorable to you. You should not be discouraged by this. It happens with everybody. You cannot be any exception of these life situations. This feel within yourself would give you a kind of psychological boost to do your best under any circumstances so that you are able to overcome any unfavorable situation. Try to understand that how can you perform the best? You can best judge your capacity to perform whenever it is so required. You would be able to bring the best out of you provided you maintain yourself as a best performer even under normal conditions. However, abnormal conditions demand some more extra efforts to continue to be the best of you. Others, who are your well wishers, can only inspire you to the best of their abilities. They cannot perform on your behalf but their sincere advice is going to help you in a manner that you will never feel alone in your life struggles. Their life experiences are much valuable. You can well learn from their experiences to accelerate your action towards best achievements. How can you get best from you that are significant? You think upon it with your cool mind and look for the measures which you can conveniently apply at your disposal. Your mind is going to be the prime factor behind your best performance. Your mind starts analyzing the related situations and circumstances which could be quite relevant in achieving that task before you. The obstacles you happen to identify on your way to best performance are to be removed first. There could be lot many obstacles which are unseen; you need to be more alert and mentally prepared about. Your mind finally takes a decision and makes signals to you whether to proceed or wait for an opportune time.

You have options to remain an average person. You may be feeling satisfied with whatever little possessions you have. But your mind never accepts this attitude. You might have noticed this behavior of your mind on number of occasions when it keeps on stimulating you from within to do your best and be the best. But what goes wrong? You wanted to be the best but you had to compromise to be among the average ones. But how did you accept that? It is a big question in the sense that you wanted to be the best. This also becomes quite significant knowing to the fact that you were much aware of your capacity to do things in best possible way. And that you were doing the things exactly like that only. Never be disheartened for things not happening according to your expectations. It so happens with those who deserve to be the actual winners. While in your pursuit to be the winner, any compromising attitude in this regard should not be any consideration. Your failures should make you strong. Any element of compromise as a remedy for such failures is not welcome. You will go much ahead from being the best.

Never forget that failures are always rewarding provided one has to pass through rigors of life to get the best. To be the best and to be on top of the world is your mental aptitude. Then why to compromise at all? Make this world known that you are the best. And that you are born to win. What is best in you is your attitude which inspires to perform and gives the most satisfaction to you. You should remain satisfied with what you do and what you get, with a never to give up approach. It may be money for some people but your satisfaction may be just the opposite not much money but just that money which fits your aims and objects of life. Feel all the best to you.

*"You have options to remain an average person. To be the best and to be on top of the world is your mental aptitude. By being the best make this world known that you are born to win. Your failures should make you strong. Any element of compromise as a remedy for such failures should not be welcome. Then you will go far away from being the best. Failure are rewarding provided you pass through rigors of life to get the best. Feel all the best to you."*

---

# 57

## CONSISTENT TEMPER

Consistency in your temper is going to be an asset for you. It is a kind of individual balancing mechanism between a temper which is good and a temper which is not good. There is very technical and attitudinal distinction between a temper which is not good and a bad temper. The tempers not good being incidental could very easily be adjusted to make it consistent with but bad tempers being intentional are very difficult in balancing and become personal behavioral trait. We often listen that there are people who are of good temperament. There are people of bad temperament as well. Of good temper or bad temper is nothing but a state of mind of a person. Always be in good temper despite the fact that few people make efforts to disturb your temper. Human mind has the capacity to maintain good temper at its own sweet will. There are people with good temper around you. They are the best with whom you feel better to associate with and to make your temper more consistent. You can achieve consistency in your temper by a regular practice and by not allowing any such thought which goes to disturb you. You are a visionary person then you need a consistently good temper to translate your visions into reality. Your temper is your possession and being in good temper is your domain. No other person has any authority to divert your attention from your domain.

What is consistent temper? Consistency of your temper could well be a stage in which your mind is so settled with positivity that it confers a permanency with flow of such ideas. When reached this stage you do not feel to exert much on your mind and it works so easy beyond your imaginations. You are going to attain this consistency of your mind by working upon it through perseverance. It could be a rigorous process but it does not mean that it is going to be a tiring process. In chemical sciences we use a term 'saturation point' which is a stage of chemical reaction in which any solution becomes saturated. When the solution is processed with certain chemicals, it keeps dissolving immediately but the moment it reached to the point of saturation, it stops reacting with no dissolution. Your temper, your mental attitude should react like this only. Make your mind so saturated with positive thoughts that it reaches to the point of saturation and stops reacting, by refusing to accept negative thoughts from others. This is when you start behaving with consistent temper. Now you do not react to unnecessary talks of others. Whenever you feel the need to be answered, you react with full consistency and command. You have left no room behind for any negative thoughts. If there happens to be any negativity around, you get it all dissolved away, to the point of saturation within your mind. That is your consistent temper.

Maintaining consistency of one's temper would be individual responsibility of the person. You should never expect the other individual is going to help you in any manner to maintain your consistency. Those who are roaming around with disturbed minds are completely unable to contribute to your consistent temper. So be master of you. Try to be always cool and calm. Avoid company of such people who are negative. They will damage consistency of your temper. Learn this habit to not to blaming others that they disturbed you. In fact you permitted them to disturb you, by letting them come close to you. It should be the strength of your consistency that they could not succeed to disturb you. Keep yourself with good and pleasant humor which enhances your capacity to perform and yields better results for your consistent temper.

*"Consistent temper is your asset to be cool and calm. Human mind has the capacity to maintain its good temper on its own sweet will. In chemical sciences we use a term 'saturation point' which is a stage of chemical reaction. When the solution is processed with, it keeps dissolving immediately but the moment it reached to the point of saturation it stops reacting with no dissolution. Your temper should also be like this only in rejecting negativity."*

---

# 58

## FORGIVE OTHERS

Forgiveness is the best human trait. People who forgive others are the great people in the sense that they practice forgiveness by keeping a big heart. Looking to the common human psychology and related behavioral patterns it is very difficult for us to forgive others for their wrongful acts. It comes in direct conflict with individual human ego when people refuse to forgive others. Consistent temper is going to play a very significant role in mental preparedness of an individual to forgive others. When one reaches to the stage of forgiveness? Someone provokes another person and the other person starts losing his temper. The other person does wrong and intentionally causing harm to someone. The person gets angry for the wrongful behavior and the harm so caused. Losing of temper is very easy for a man who is not able to balance his temper. What should he do now? He should burst out of anger and start crying on the other man. Or he should keep silent. Be sure, the other man despite being on wrong footing, is also going to cry in similar tone. Bursting out of anger is easy but it is not advisable. One can burst even without a trace of anger. This trait of forgiveness has been very nicely devised for protecting us from harmful effects of anger. To be in anger would be damaging to your health. That is also true that there are people who are not going to listen to your polite words and making you to lose your temper.

This may damage your administrative image and productivity of your organization too. Politeness could be for the people who are equally polite and are ready to understand the things. But what about the people who refuse to be polite? Here lies the real problem but at the same time it affords an opportunity to you to practice your trait of forgiving others. Let the politeness be your habit and it inculcates through your actions and reactions.

Your politeness should not be taken as your weakness. Your forgiveness too should not be considered to be your weakness. There are people who are going to consider your preparedness to forgive others as your weakness. Even if you happen to forgive them, they are in their habit to disturb you. Playing with reputation and lowering status of others is also very common. Keeping balance in such an event is very difficult. This is going to be your testing time and you have to be emerged victorious. Your greatness lies in the fact that despite all opposed situations, without losing your temper, you forgive others. This is a very highest mental stage of a man, which is not that easy for everybody to attain with. In such situations feel the struggle going inside you? You are a sensible man with all due regard to human sensitivities. You observe the chain of thoughts which are coming to your mind at that moment. Either you are going to forgive him or you decide not to forgive. You experience the relief of your mind you are getting, when you decide to forgive the other man. Of course they have committed mistakes but your greatness is in forgetting all about. Let them realize that they committed mistake. They would realize one day if not today that despite all that you forgave them. But you keep acting upon the way you feel to be fair on your part. They keep watching you and your approach towards others. They would find that come what may, you practice forgiveness. They are compelled to be overwhelmed by your attitude. Never leave your attitude to forgive it pays in long run in fulfilling your life objectives. One day you would see that you have emerged victorious and have won over them, who used to commit mistakes and you forgave. Your attitude of forgiveness changed them completely. This is the strength of forgiveness. It would change our social morality and fill it with total happiness.

*"Forgiveness is the best human trait. People forgiving others are great. Bursting out of anger is not advisable. Neither your politeness nor your forgiveness should be taken as your weakness by others. You experience the relief of your mind when you forgive. Your attitude of forgiveness would reform them completely coming across a changed social morality and fill it with total happiness."*

# 59

## ALWAYS THINK BIG

Thinking big is an inbuilt character of the people who are destined to be great. Human minds have thinking patterns as distinguished from animals. This is either conferred by the nature to a man or else the man himself develops this character with the passage of time. A man should always think big. A man desires to do big things in his life. As an aspirant if you want to be a big achiever then you would have to think big otherwise you will not be in a position to achieve big in your life. Always think world class. Dreaming big has its proportional co-relationship with thinking big. Make your dreams high you will see that you are compelled to think high, so as to get your dreams fulfilled. No doubt thinking big is the first step towards becoming big. Every big initiative of your life starts with your thinking mind. You start thinking first and chalk out your plans accordingly. Thinking big would be followed by you to work upon it. This must be called as initiating the process in implementing your ideas into reality. Your thoughts should not be limited to your mind or left written behind on papers only. Unless the plans of your thinking mind are drawn at the grass roots levels, thinking big would be of no use.

First, let us properly understand as to what do we mean by thinking big? Whether thinking big for own self if one happens to be individualistic? Or thinking big for the people at large as well if one happens to be collective? Bigness of ideas lies in the fact that they are some way or the other for the welfare of the mankind. Such ideas emphasize that prosperity prevails at large and people live with love and brotherhood for each other. There prevails feeling of humanism among people with all due respect to human sensibilities. You can think big in terms of your career that you wish to be at the heights of glory. You want to be a big business man, so you think big to earn big and get richer. Earning money by whatever means is easy but retaining that money in a good spirit is very difficult. We have witnessed such business people who are after money by whatever means and become multimillionaires overnight. But the moment their empire starts collapsing they are left with nowhere. The day comes when you feel that you have earned enough money to satisfy your material needs. You have surplus money left behind and you decided to extend financial help to other people who are destitute and are in dire need of money. You emerged as a divine figure for them. You never think of any such certificates given to you since it is your inner conscience which gives you the certificate.

Charity always begins at home. Not that money only could be the method, to do for the betterment of public at large. You think to be the part of state governance system and to serve the people better the way you think to be keeping in mind the resources. If good, dedicated and honest people are not willing to join public life then the field of state governance is left wide open for wrongdoers and incapables. Bad governance as a result is not to be blamed then. There are such situations what the state governance is facing today. Deteriorating law and order problems, increasing unemployment conditions, people suffering from poor health due to poverty, public education absolutely going in bad shape, are some of the features of serious concern which our society today is painfully struggling from. We cannot look for any excuse that there is nothing much to think big.

*"Thinking big is an inbuilt character for the men who are destined to be great. Dreaming big has its proportional co-relationship with thinking big. No doubt thinking big is the first*

*step towards becoming big. Every big initiative of your life starts with your thinking mind. Earning money by whatever means is easy but retaining that money in a good spirit is very difficult. We cannot overlook the matters of social concern like public health, education and unemployment. There would be no excuse for us to say that there was nothing much to think big. Humanism prevails with thinking human sensibilities."*

# 60

## CONTROLLING YOUR MIND

Your mind is a powerful machine and it is the powerhouse of your body system. You must be surprised to know that a small part inside the head of human body contains such power that it needs to be properly controlled and channelized. It controls and regulates the bodily activities of all living beings. Since it is considered that human mind is much developed therefore human beings are supposed to be strong and better civilized. Strength of your mind has been linked with your thinking capacity. Better you think, better you are. You start thinking bad you are bound to face badly, sooner or later. It is said that your thoughts decide your destiny. Thus it becomes very essential for you to develop a kind of controlling mechanism so that you achieve the targets in your life what you are looking for. Do we feel that our mind needs to be properly controlled and regulated? If you happen to mark the speed of your mind you will find that it runs with a very fast pace. At one point of time you will find that it is roaming around in Delhi, the capital city of India and just in the next moment in fraction of seconds it reaches to the love city of Paris, the capital of France. See the fast speed of your mind that physically you are in India but mentally you are in France, which is thousands of miles away. And your mind reaches there within fraction of seconds. What does it mean? Are you able to control your mind? If not, then you are going to fail in controlling your mind and as a result failing in concentration of mind. You are preparing for competitions which need concentration. You will find that you are trying very tough to concentrate your eyes on the subject matter in the book while your mind is jumping jack in hills with your sweet heart.

How can you develop the controlling mechanism this is worth understanding? Whenever you focus a target to hit, you need a mind with full concentration. The process of controlling your mind is a difficult task, no doubt, but it is not impossible. You need a stable mind to concentrate with. A disturbed mind cannot attain the state of stability. When your mind gets disturbed? Try to identify and pin point those factors. Are you able to notice those factors which are instrumental in disturbing you, where you fail to control your mind? Simple way out is that once you are able to identify those factors which disturb the concentration of your mind, you make efforts to prevent those factors from entering into your mind. Undoubtedly, this is not an easy task and this is not going to happen overnight. It may take a long time with your honest and regular practicing. But it would happen definitely one day and you would be able to control your mind.

My only intention is that you should utilize the energy of your power house in the best possible manner to achieve your life objectives. There are two possibilities. Either you control your mind or let the mind control you. Establish your control over mind so that you are successfully able to channelize the mind energy towards desired directions. Think better, do better, your mind is going to be controlled automatically. Make this world a better place for you to live in and for others as well. A controlled mind always thinks in manner, to work for best possible results. It enhances your decision making capacity in a much sharper way so that you are in a position to tackle with the obstacles very easily. While encountering with adverse conditions your controlled mind helps you much in keeping you stable with your action and reactions. Your positive thoughts help you to control your mind in a positive manner leading to concentration of mind for all the times.

*"Your mind is a powerful machine. It runs at a very fast speed, so it needs proper controlling mechanism to channelize with, in desired directions. Either you control your mind or let the mind control you. Better you think, better you are. It is true that your thoughts decide your destiny. A controlled mind always thinks in a manner to work for best possible results. You develop a controlling mechanism of your mind so that you are able to reach up to your targets even encountering through most adverse conditions in your life."*

---

# 61

## EARN YOUR KNOWLEDGE

Knowledge cannot not be inherited through transfer of chromosomal genes from one generation to the other generation. One has to earn knowledge by putting in hard work throughout. A doctor cannot transfer his meritorious knowledge to his children. Similarly an advocate can transfer his clientage to his children but will not be able to transfer his meritorious knowledge genetically. You are active because you have proper knowledge. You have proper knowledge because you have earned it. You will be lesser active due to lack of knowledge. You will go weak because you are depending upon knowledge of others. There is a famous proverb that knowledge is power. It strengthens you and helps in sharpening your mind. People with sharp mind are rare. They make it sharper by practicing more. This is not by birth but people develop sharpness of their mind to keep practicing upon it through knowledge. Earning knowledge for them is more significant for success rather than being dependent on the knowledge of others. Once you are going to earn your knowledge it will make you express it with full confidence. If for the purpose of your decision making, you are looking for the knowledge from somebody else, then be sure there are possibilities of your decision going defective or wrong, unless the person on whom you are depending upon is exceptionally trustworthy.

In today's world of dishonesty and moral degradation it is very difficult to get credible men for whatsoever purpose. Experience of elderly responsible could be the best source of acquiring fair knowledge. Books could be your best friends on which you can rely the most. Always be careful in choosing good books which are richer in quality and its contents. Your worldly day to day experience enhances your knowledge in much practical way provided you are seriously working upon it. Experience based knowledge is the real knowledge for a person since this comes out of his day to day practical life. He does some acts, commits errors then rectifies his errors and learns about it. It is said that learning by doing is more fruitful. This is because the man has to apply his knowledge according to the situations and the circumstances of life he has been put in. His situations may be unique so he needs to handle them in a unique manner. This way whatever the practical knowledge he earns is also unparallel and would be helpful to others when they fall in similar situations in their different stages of life. It is true that knowledge which one learns through experience in life is not available in book. In nutshell, so work, face hardships, apply your mind, then learn and earn your knowledge.

I would ask one question from you. It is a very practical question. How do you feel when you are acting upon your knowledge? Full with confidence…!!! Why not? It is true that when we proceed with the help of our personal knowledge and not borrowed one then our head is held high with enriched determination and confidence. Chances of any errors in decisions are very rare when you act the way your mind thinks and by applying your knowledge. Never feel disheartened if your knowledge is not that diversified but your decisions are going to be upright. You are given with responsibilities quite at an early stage when you are lacking with practical knowledge. Never mind, go on handling your responsibilities honestly. You will gain knowledge gradually but steady. You earn it by your worldly experience and complete that. Time is the best teacher for you. It teaches you the knowledge which may not be available in books. You will learn it with passage of time.

*"Knowledge is not inherited through chromosomal transfer but it is earned by putting in hard work. It gives you power to tackle life adversities. Books could be your best friends for acquiring knowledge. Honestly rely them most. The experience based knowledge you earn is not available in books. Elderly responsible knowledge is of great value. Always be careful in choosing good books which are richer in quality and its contents. Your worldly day to day experience enhances your knowledge in much practical way."*

---

# 62

## DO NOT HATE

Feeling of love and feeling of hatred are the two equally sensible but just opposite dimensions of human psyche. Loving people is positive while hating is negative. Love generates affection and closeness while hate gives to hatred and distancing between the people. Spreading of love and affection must be the purpose of life but we witness just the opposite in given society. Why the feeling of hatred among individuals? This question is quite painful and makes one to see across his inner conscience. You are a progressive minded person and getting successful too. People in society do not like to see that you are progressing. They may go jealous about your success. You are going to feel very bad about it looking to their jealousy. This is the time when you have to apply your progressive mind. Let them be jealous but you should not hate them. Why people go jealous about you? It is a very narrow thinking pattern of human mind. You should not go wasting your precious time in searching any answer to this question. It is their negative mindset. That is not your problem, so you should not be worried about it. You are riding on progressive steps so you work upon it. It's human psychology that people do not like success of other man unless they are truly close to him. You do not hate them, may be this helps in changing their mindset. To hate is negative, so you do not be negative.

You are right that in practice it is very difficult. But in my opinion it is not going to be any big problem for you. Why do you think so? Where is the problem in fact? Even in practice it is not that difficult the way you think. If people are in the habit of being jealous to somebody then that is their problem. The point is that you should completely remain unaffected by this. You can stay very much amidst such people with your identity intact. You think whether you are honest to yourself? Answer comes in affirmative. You are honest to your convictions. Then it is going to be quite certain that you would be honest to others as well. Then where is the problem? You will be honest to such people also who are jealous to you. You just control your behavior. You take care that you should not see them with any jealousy or hate. Being not hateful to them at the same time you have to be quite alert also. Such people may take undue advantage of your generosity or kindness. No one should attempt to overpower you because you are kind to them. The people who are jealous to you may harm you also. Be kind to them but be careful at the same time. Without diverting your attention you just concentrate to your business.

Sadistic pleasure is for those who are negative. It is in the sense when you are not successful in your life projects then such people are going to enjoy it. They would feel happy when some harm has occurred to you. Looking to their negative behavior you should try to control yourself without expressing displeasure of any kind towards them. By your regular positive responses if you are able to change their mindset to think differently than it is well and good. You are definitely giving them a message which would change their thinking patterns in due course of time. One day you will notice that your continuous generous behavior compels them to feel repent and makes them to change themselves. Consider it as your big achievement since you have successfully changed their negativity. Society could be changed from negativity to positivity by means of your good behavior. Society is by and large of good people. We need to bring them on a common plate form for a better world not by hate but by love and affection.

*"Love brings closeness while hate generates distancing. To hate is negative, so you do not be negative. Spreading of love and affection must be the purpose of life. Love generates affection and closeness. Let people be jealous about you but you should not hate them. It is definitely a tough time for you to control yourself. By your positive response if you are able to change them to think differently than it is well and good. You are definitely giving them a message which would change their thinking patterns in due course of time."*

---

# **63**

## WELCOME CRITICS

Criticisms are not in good taste to people. It is said that we should welcome critics and their criticism. It becomes very difficult at times to decide whether criticisms should be taken in positive taste or negative. It goes quite negative to those who do not like it. But still they are advised by the motivational thinkers that they should receive in good taste. Critics are the best tools for one's personality development. Do not take criticism as anything adverse for you. They with all good intentions pin point certain drawbacks in your personality by way of criticizing you. Take it in positive sense since it may prove to be an improvement in your personality. There are people who keep on criticizing everybody. You do not bother for such people as they do it by their habit. Such people are problematic with complete negative approach. You should not take their criticisms by your heart as they are very cheap by their thinking. But try to identify those critics who are your well-wishers and they are honest about you. They while criticizing you indicate few of your weakness, with a good intention to make you a better performer. Critics are just opposite to sycophants. As compared to critics, the sycophants by keep pleasing you may put you in trouble some day. But in case of critics there is no such possibility at least, because while criticizing they keep at a distance from you.

You need to accept your criticisms honestly and analyze it with a view to remove those weaknesses in your actions. Critics could basically be put into two categories. First types are those who criticize you with all malice to discourage you, so that you lose your confidence and harm is caused to you. They also intend for loss of your reputation in the society. Such critics are very easily identifiable. They may appear to be quite good to you as your well-wisher. You may be confused by their outwardly behavior as to how come they can do any wrong to you? But they do, that is the real problem. Their behavior used to be so polite and caring that you were quite impressed about it. They are not critical to you in front of you but they prove to be quite damaging from behind your back. By means of a little bit alert mind, you would be able to identify such people. By being in this society you cannot avoid such people interacting with you. No problem. Interact with them openly but never be close to them. By keeping at a distance from them you are alert but the moment you are getting close to them, you are giving them a ready chance to harm you.

The second category of critics is of the people who criticize your work with all their bonafide deep heart. By criticizing you they never intend to lower your morale or in any way to disrespect you. On the other hand they desire that you should improve upon your errors and keep progressing in your career. They honestly see the kind of possibilities of achievements in you, looking to your merit and sincerity. They may appear to be not so polite to you, look to be rude but they are honest. They are visibly critical in front of you only without bothering for whether you may feel bad about. They will speak out everything before you. You may feel bad for a moment but always remember that such people are never going to be harmful to you. It is their honesty for your wellness which they are not able to conceal. They may be critical but they prove to be quite helpful to you. Welcome them and keep by your side. You can rely upon them because such people are open hearted and trust worthy.

*"Criticisms are not in good taste. Critics are the best tools for one's personality development. Do not take criticism as anything adverse for you. Honest critics do it with all good intentions to see the kind of improvement you are lacking in. They while criticizing you pin point few of your weaknesses with a good intention to make you better performer. There are critics who criticize you with all malice against you. You should not bother about them at all. Welcome honest critics who speak the truth about you and keep them by your side."*

# 64

## FOR A NOBLE CAUSE

You are born in this world for a noble cause, of thinking about and doing about welfare of the mankind on this earth. Your being in this world has a meaning. By your actions you have to make it to be more meaningful. Do you remember this world when you were a small kid? How beautiful this world used to be in your childhood? Pleasant memories of your childhood must be still fresh in your mind. You were an honest witness to, what all was happening in this world. How do you feel today when you happen to remember those happiest days when you were free from all worries? When you used to keep running behind tiny butterflies, all the day? Sometimes you were able to catch them, sometimes not. Even then you were not discouraged. You kept waiting for other butterflies to come around. Once, while catching butterflies you fell down badly and suffered injuries. Nobody was there to help you get up. You had to manage yourself to get up with sheer pain, then to run again because there were butterflies. This world was so beautiful for you and this life too, with pleasant memories.

Now you were getting young with a feel of responsibility. The kind of responsibilities you were never able to understand. You also had the feel of responsibility, probably of your being in this world. You still while young, watched that the butterflies were around but you did not feel like to start running behind them, catch them. Just sitting and kept watching them joyfully and letting them go. Now see the change of your mindset, while letting them go has been more joyful to you, instead of catching them. Your perception towards this world was changing with a sense of responsibility being infused inside you. Slowly and slowly you were developing deep understanding for this world. You felt concerned about for everything which was wrongful and adversely affected any innocent one. It was painful for you though it did not harm you anyway. Your heart comes out full with grief and starts crying for all that what used to be unjust and unfair. You were full with worries when you were not able to undo the wrongs being done by others for their own vested interests,

See...!!! This would go as an endless worry for you since you are not a self-centered man. When people say why to worry? Was it not completely inhuman? How the people are so tough hearted to turn a blind eye for the problems of their fellow citizen? You considered it to be an escapist tendency of such people. They made a paradise of their own and being least bothered about rest of the innocent underprivileged people on this earth. Make it a point that your concern for them is going to make you strong with a determination to do something to protect their interest. Today you don't find yourself able to do something to undo the wrongs done to them. You wanted to help them but your financial condition was not good. You thought that they could be given proper education so that they could be self dependant. This was the best what you could do to them. But that was not all going to be sufficient for them. Their concern inspired you from within to make yourself capable enough one day, to win over your worries by doing for them what they were supposed to be done for, by the caretakers of this system. Looking to the big number of such needy people, you understand that what you are doing is much less about it. But still you have the confidence that your life could contribute, even for a small bit, to the noble cause of the people who are in need.

*"You are born in this world for a noble cause to thinking and doing about welfare of the mankind. You have your perception towards betterment of this world. Your being in this world has a meaning. You are concerned about the people who are in need. With your limited resources you decided to help them. You have the confidence that your life could contribute even for a small bit to the noble cause and that was the goal of your life. The concern for such people in your mind inspires you to make yourself capable to win over your worries for them."*

---

# 65

# YOUR PERSONALITY REFLECTS

What is personal to you? Being quite personal to you, still it influences others. That should be your personality. What you think within yourself, you do not speak out. You keep silent. But your body language makes all the difference. It speaks loud and clear. The way you move, the way you dress yourself and express your ideas among people. The way you walk and the way you talk, it reflects. Whether you prefer to keep silent or speak, it makes its own impact upon people. It may sound strange but true that a person's silence also speaks a lot. It has become your habit that you speak much less. People also do know about it. But when you speak, your words carry weight. Your lesser words carry bigger meaning. People respect your silence. They mean it. Being talkative also would be of no sense if people have no respect for your words. Being more talkative fails to reflect sound, at the same time it mars your personality. What to speak? When to speak and how much to speak? It is an important trait of human personality.

Today's era, even if it is commercial and materialistic but it is an era of good will. People in commercial activities are not successful if they do not act well to their customers with their smiling faces. Who is going to assess your personality, is rather less significant then what do you think about your personality to be? Today is also an era of flow of knowledge and information. Acquiring knowledge is a tedious task but once you are able to get into the task, brightness of it could well be seen in your personality as a moving institution. Every person's personality is unique in itself. You need to maintain a striking balance between demand of the hour and the need of the hour. You may think differently but in your profession you have to develop your personality as per the requirements of your business and according to the taste of your customers. The demand of the hour could be much less in number, only for the chosen few who can afford and make demands. But you need to keep an eye for the larger common good. Developing your personality according to the demand of the hour may appear to be commercial but while you perceive yourself and advance according to the need of the people you become strong in your reflection and attitude.

A stage comes in your life when you feel that you should contribute for others, those who are in need and are socially, educationally and economically weak. Then nothing remains personal for you. Your personality becomes public. You feel since you also struggled through similar situations and circumstances. You are able to connect your personality with them. Now people also start connecting with you and identify themselves with your personality. Your personality gets merged with the personality of the people at large. You may feel whether you are up to support them by whatever means you are able to do. No problem. Your dedicated moral support merely, gives them the needed strength so that they make themselves to stand upright. Your personality not only reflects but infuses in them the confidence that you are there behind them standing as a rock. What if, one lives for himself? See, the one who lives for others. You have to just develop a feel of the kind. Your personality would be automatically transformed like that only. You would sense the greatness in serving others. That is the virtual reflection. Live up to that. You would find that you have accomplished the mission for your life.

*"Your personality speaks louder and clear. People respect your silence. But when you speak your words carry weight. Your*

*lesser words carry bigger meaning. You may think differently but in your profession you have to develop your personality as per the requirements of your business and according to the taste of your customers. Demand may be of chosen few but you need to keep an eye for the larger common good. You need to maintain a striking balance between demand of the hour and the need of the hour. When you connect yourself for a common good then your personality becomes public."*

———————————————————

# 66

# BODY LANGUAGE

You are presenting yourself before the interview board with a smiling face. There is no sign of disappointment while you are talking and responding to the queries put to you by the subject experts. While you entered into the room for interview your balanced steps were reflecting the confidence inside. You reached up to the interview table waiting for a moment, till you are asked to take your chair. While you moved inside the interview room and occupied the chair, every movement of yours was being watched very carefully by the members of the interview board. Your body language made the first impression about the confidence level you had while you were about to be interviewed. And first impression is the last impression, you know. Your confidence had to be there quite automatically because your mind was full with information. This goes to show that reflection of the confidence in your body language has been proportionally related with quantum of knowledge you carry. This knowledge could be purely of the nature of trade and profession you are engaged in.

The nature of information for a sportsperson would be quite different from the nature of the information which is expected from a philosopher. But both are the stalwarts of their fields and both possess body language of their own profession they are putting in. A farmer would have his own body language full with command though he may not be much literate. A person who is rich with material resources gets a boost in enhancing the confidence through his body language. Educated and knowledgeable persons would have a different kind of confidence levels which any amount of money cannot purchase. Health is wealth. You can well understand the role of a healthy body in your body language. A healthy body possesses a healthy mind. With clarity of thoughts and sharpness, your mind would be in much commanding position to control your body language accurately at a particular point of time. One should not forget that money earned by improper means breads completely different kind of body language which does not always help the person. But this is not applicable in case of the body language which reflects in persons who are learned. Body language which is due to the result of education and learning is always on the much higher side in the sense that it always keeps you within manners and goodness. This is always positive and progressive.

You should always keep this fact in mind as to how your body language would be helpful in advancing your future prospects? May be you are in business or a practicing lawyer. You are preparing for competitive examinations and you have to appear before the interview board. You are determined to clear the interview by expressing your knowledge while your body language simultaneously enhances your confidence at that time. As an advocate while you are arguing your case before the court, at the same time with the help of your expressions through your body language, you are successfully in a position to impress upon the court regards to the gravity of the matter you are arguing. This would help you in getting the judicial order in favor of your client. Life itself is a big journey in which you will encounter with various adversities and negative personalities. Your aggressive body language would defeat the malicious intentions of your opponents at the same time your softness would attract your supporters to make you more strong. Always move ahead with your body language intact. It is your asset. Protect and conserve it, in your day to day life, not only for yourself but in the interest of your fellow citizen as well.

*"Always move ahead with your body language intact. It is a lifetime asset for you. One can well understand the role of healthy body in his impressive body language. Your body language made the first impression about your confidence level you had at the time of interview. Your education and knowledge helps in enhancing your confidence. You are determined to clear your interview. Your aggressive body language would defeat malice of your opponents."*

---

# **67**

## YOU ARE BY CHOICE

You prepare hard and work hard in your life but you find that despite your sincere efforts you failed. You wanted to join civil services. You understand that it is just not going to happen like that. It needed a lot of preparation day and night to take on the subjects and other related studies. You wanted to be a judge. That was your choice. Looking the preparation for judgeship it was altogether a complete switch over of discipline for the subjects of legal sciences. You started preparation with the same vigor for hours of studies untiring. But you could not get through that even. It never meant that you did not possess the required knowledge. In a competitive field it happens that others could prove themselves to be more suitable for that position. You just lagged behind little bit. That's all. Now you are not going to sit idle. You would start preparing for other avenues. You may feel disappointed for the reasons that you could not get the positions what you wanted. Disappointment is quite natural because it is a normal state of mind for every individual. But you need to be careful that this mindset is not going to overpower you. Never allow frustration or depression to control your mind. It is going to make you a weak person and would harm you.

To be more confident and successful in your life it is always better that never to confine yourself to any single choice. Though this may sound good but goes much difficult in practice. Advising one to go for medical studies and at the same time trying for engineering courses would definitely be a difficult exercise. Right in the beginning the students decide with a certain streams of their choice studies to pursue with. But looking to the existing competitive scenario with limited avenues available, not all are going to get the streams of their choice. Obviously the youngsters are going to be disappointed since they could not succeed despite they put in their sincere hard work. Such kinds of uncertainties are always to be kept in mind for a safer take. Keep yourself psychologically prepared for more than one alternative choice. You will not feel involved and comfortable in your life unless you go in a profession of your choice. On occasions you would feel that you are not by choice but you are by chance. This feeling is also not much good because you will find yourself to be not in a position to involve yourself completely in a job which is not by your choice. Make it a point that if you are not working hard to get a future of your choice than ultimately you will be forced to go for a career which you got by chance.

There are famous sayings that you work hard to get, what you wish otherwise you will be forced to accept, what you get. There is nothing by chance. It is always by your choice, something less or something more. You agree to settle yourself with what you get under the circumstances. May be you are not able to get exactly what you wished to be. You just missed your choice by a few margin. You had an option to keep repeating to write the same competition or to switch over to any other stream of your second choice as per your eligibility criteria. But still under such calling circumstances you never lost your confidence and kept working hard. You never wanted to be a loser in your life by any means whatsoever. What you got subsequently that was also by your choice since you had to accept that in absence of your better first choice. Never complaint and blame others for whatever you get in your life. Keep working for your ultimate choice in a best possible manner. And your ultimate choice of life is to be a better human being with peace of your mind and happiness.

*"You could not succeed does not mean that you did not possess the required knowledge. You just lagged behind by a little bit margins. Looking to the volume of competition and limited choice avenues you need to have alternative choices well in advance in your mind. You are always by your choice, something less or something more. Work hard to get what you wish otherwise you will be forced to accept what you get. Keep working for your ultimate choice in a best possible manner. And your ultimate choice is to be a better human being."*

---

# 68

## HONESTY OF WORDS

Words have power and they carry weight. Words have mass and they have their own meaning to forcefully convey. One becomes very aggressive on occasions and he communicates such mindset by means of using such words of aggression. People are very submissive and polite also by the soft words they speak while communicating with people. A person while making any statement or communication with others displays his power or authority by means of using words of that nature. You are always supposed to be honest while you speak and thereafter when you are expected to honor your words already spoken. While speaking either in public or even otherwise you are expected to be very careful and cautious in choosing your words. Once the words are spoken it is impossible for you to take them back. Even if you feel sorry later for your foul words and express your apology but the wrong has already been which now cannot be undone. Relations thus so spoiled become very difficult to carry on. Giving words in one's life are very easy than keeping those words in the same spirit. It always becomes a question of your own credibility when you happen to make certain promises but you fail to keep your words. Your honesty is reflected by words in your personality. Your body has its own language to speak out with kind of the words which are very easily understandable. Keeping honest is not a much difficult task for a person provided he has his own convictions to follow with complete commitment. One simply needs a firm determination to be honest. Making a determination is also very simple but it needs a rigorous practice to reach upon and to retain that in your mind and converting it into your life style.

A very disturbing question may come up in your mind. Why to make extra efforts to maintain honesty particularly in a world which is going full with dishonesty? That is true. When people appear to be abusive as a very common practice, then those respecting their words against them start losing their patient. Yes…!!! This could be a question which needs many considerations. The people, who sincerely try to be honest with their words and deeds, go discouraged by an atmosphere of dishonesty all around them. The question to be answered with any haste is undoubtedly difficult. You being honest that is your personal commitment and a kind of pledge to your inner conscience. But at the same time expecting others to be equally honest could be disappointing. Practicing honesty with your words could be at times difficult, whereas people are attracted towards dishonesty for the reasons that it has short term easy dividends. They are tempted by such small gains which is quite psychological.

Now what to do under such circumstances? The choice is completely yours. Honesty of your words enhances your credibility amongst masses and it attaches with you as a body impersonate. Thus without getting much worried about, you continue to pursue your belief in honesty with your words. You become a force to reckon with. People believe in you for keeping your words meticulously. They make their important decisions relying upon your words and they become successful in their pursuits. You become much valuable in their life events. This has got more meaning to your life objectives. Mind it, one is going to get some short term easy gains by resorting to dishonest means but honesty to your words guarantees you a permanent long term gains in your life. For all that you need a consistency in your patience. My humble advice would be that go for a long term permanent gain. Life would welcome you.

*"Words have power and they carry weight. You are honest to your words when you go on to keep your words with due respects. You have to be very careful in choosing your words because once spoken, words cannot be taken back. Giving words in one's life is very easy than keeping those words in the same spirit. It becomes a question of credibility if you fail to keep your words. Your honesty is reflected by your words in your personality."*

———————————————————

# 69

# THINGS RIGHT AND JUST

It is never ever necessary that only the persons who are literate would be in a position to adjudge whether what is right, just and fair? You can observe feelings of justness and fairness in the pronouncements of people who are just illiterate. It is their sense of perception as to what is right and just and the same has no link with any educational qualification. No doubt literacy gives one, richness of thoughts and a vision to plan with but it has no direct relationship with the fact that a person who is literate would be right and just essentially. You will experience that literate persons are seen doing unjust acts and taking wrongful decisions which cannot be said to be any human error. My personal study in this respect shows that the people who are illiterate are comparatively more sensible to do the things in a rightful and just manner. Not all but those who become literate look to be at times more deliberate and careless. My submission should be taken as mark of perception whereas common minimum literacy campaigns remain basic need of the hour.

It has become a painful tendency of the day that people who are educated seen to be cleverer in developing tactful devices in doing right things, in a wrongful manner and by wrongful means. The obvious motive behind all that is wrongful gain for them. The very objective of their literacy through better education is defeated. There are numerous rampant cases of corruption in public administration fields in criminal nexus with private sectors. It is all well educated class who had been supposed to be right and just in its action but they did not. There were black spots observed in justice administration fields too. Looking to perceptions of right and justness, illiterate innocent people have comparatively an accurate and bigger sense of pity and probity.

Not only human beings even animals and birds do possess a natural tendency of responding to the situations in a right and just manner. A man was pelting stones to a dog in the street. The dog had the right sense, to bark at the man who was pelting stones instead chasing for stones. When cats are seen around the bird's nest, you can witness the birds collectively chasing the cat away. They could sense the things which were not right. It could be simply described as neutrality of justice in the sense that we are born to be just and fair on this earth. Justness flows by its nature. Be it a human being or an animal. You notice sometime yourself honestly. When you were unjust and acted wrongfully, you were feeling not comfortable for many days. It is different that you went to suppress your emotions against the postures of neutrality of justness.

If our educated literacy had to have some meaning then we need to identify such factors which are responsible for spoiling the very nature of a man which went wrong and unjust. You observe minutely and you will find that nature is always just and fair. Same is also right with human nature. Watch carefully, whenever human mind goes against its nature and thinks wrongfully intending to do something unfair, his inner conscience hits him back as if stopping him from doing that act. We develop tendencies and our own justifications to ignore this inner voice. A stage arrives in our life that one day we reach to a point of no return. Feeling of repentance would also be of no meaning since a lot of damage was already done due to our wrongful acts. This is going to disturb peace of your mind. Problem starts for you the moment you started manipulating things and you went wrong in your doings. You didn't rectify even when it comes to your notice. This is deliberate. You just buy peace for your mind by remaining right and just in your acts. Remember that one day would come in your life when you would repent to your wrongful and unfair deeds but it would be too late then.

*"No doubt literacy gives one, richness of thoughts and a vision to plan with but it has no direct relationship with the fact that a person who is literate would be right and just essentially. My personal observation is that the people who are illiterate are comparatively more sensible to do the things in a rightful and just manner."*

———————————————————

# 70

## MANAGE YOUR STRESS

In the present day hectic activities of the society, stress levels to human mind is very high. As if stress is to human alone. People are seen running helter skelter on the streets day and night. Some are running gainfully while others are still struggling without gain. One can understand the stress level of those who are the losers but the gainers are seen equally stressful, in their bid to further multiply their gains. This way life struggle of people goes on. Stress is harmful to your body and mind. Stress has to be there in our life, to boldly face it. Unless we develop mechanisms to manage our stress beautifully, we all will be painful losers. You must not be surprised to notice that not only the human but animals too, could be seen in stress for various reasons. Negative human behavior towards animals makes a definite impact in their change of behavior. Why stress has become to human? It needs an in depth study to properly understand this. You would feel under stress when things are not happening up to your calculations.

You worked to get something but you could not get that. You are seen that you come under stress. Yes…!!! How it is going to be certain that things are going to happen, exactly the way you want? Happening of a thing would be dependent upon the quality of efforts you have put in honestly. It may happen obviously the way you wanted provided you have put in your efforts that way. It may not happen as well despite you worked. It is the extent of human desires which are going to generate the amount of stress, one is suffering from. If a person is able to control his desires within permissible limits and keeps himself satisfied with what he gets then there is no reason that stress is going to trouble him. You may also experience a kind of negative human behavior in our society that when you lead your life happily and free from stress then the people, who are mentally crooks and envious of your happiness, start creating unnecessary trouble for you and put you under stress. You manage your stress against such people by keeping yourself positive to beat their negativity. Keep yourself alert and be aware of such people by maintaining a distance from them. Such people can't put to you under any stress, without you being close to them. Let them do what they can do. They are in the habit of it, doing with similar negativity with others as well. You just don't care about them. Stress created by them is not going to touch you.

Be clear that you are also equally responsible, for all that stress to you. Ups and downs are there in everybody's life and are going to trouble them. This only is the way of life. Life is not a bed of roses. It is full with thorns. Life troubles you at the same time it crowns you with happiness. Do not fear from stress because once you work upon, it makes you strong. Make it a point that by managing sufferings in your life you will be able to search out the peace and happiness for you. Whenever you start expecting anything for you then it is sure, you are inviting stress for yourself. You just work upon your life pursuits and let the things happen for you spontaneously. This may sound to be a very tough advice to you but still, avoid expecting anything from your children even. Do for them whatever you can and let them lead their own life. Inculcate in them human values so that they could withstand negative social pressures. The moment you started expecting from them and if for any reason they are not up to your expectations then you are down with stress. Managing your stress thus is well within your control. Never allow any stress agent to creep in your mind. Stress successfully makes room in weaker minds. Overpower your stress once and throw it out of your mind ruthlessly never to enter again.

*"Stress has to be there in our life to boldly face it. Unless we develop mechanism to manage our stress beautifully, we will be painful losers. Stress successfully makes room in weaker minds. Expectation based human desires generate stress which we need to avoid. Do not fear from stress because once you work upon, it makes you strong never to enter again in your mind."*

---

# 71

## YOU WILL NEVER FAIL

This is a success formula for your life which always keeps this confidence in your mind intact that you are born to win. No doubt, what you do is important. But that apart, with the confidence you are doing a particular work, becomes more significant in your success. Confidence building process of your mind would be depending upon the fact that what are the kinds of tools you have developed to maintain your confidence level intact? You keep sharpening your mind with the help of continuous flow of knowledge which is an essential tool in this process. You are getting yourself ready to hit the target with specific mindset. You are concentrating with your mental strength to focus your target. What is needed is that you continue with that mindset till you hit the target and reach your goal. But you feel that maintaining that mindset for all the times is not always possible. Yes...!!! You are right. That's all quite practical. Adversities keep coming in one's life, which reduce your confidence level. This is the rule of nature. All the great men on this earth had to face varieties of troubles in their life before they could achieve success in true sense and became great.

Make it a conviction in your mind that although failure may come in your life journey but you are not made for failures. There should be no word like failure in your dictionary. Failures do not mean that you could not achieve your immediate targets. But you were never disheartened by your failures and could get your ultimate goal by means of making untiring sincere efforts against all odds. What was significant for you that despite failures you never lost your confidence? Understand that success is nothing but an end product of failures provided you did not give up and stop from making efforts. Because you had the conviction in your mind that you would never fail. Conviction is a state of mind where your mind decides to perform any function with full of confidence. If it happens to be a job not that easy, your mind immediately reacts for extra efforts to be made. The needed extra efforts are to be made by you only. You understand your working potential. Now, to begin with extra efforts, it is going to be your mind again which musters the needed will power and infuses inside you, the strength to strike with at the right moment and at the right place.

The two most significant factors for a person to be successful are his mental element first and followed by his physical element. It is the mind which thinks first and comes out with an idea for a man to proceed with. Unless the man starts some physical action, it would not be possible for him to work upon that idea and come out with expected results. It would depend upon the level of sincerity the person is making, the outcome would be fast and he keeps striking with much added strength. He starts disappointing immediately if the outcome is delayed or it is not as expected. Getting disappointed is human nature. But never allow the disappointment to settle down in your mind. It will diminish your working potential and your rate of performance. This would be the success formula for you which would let you never to fail. This is going to be a testing time for you in your life. Even after failures you are not feeling disappointed. This is the strength of your mind which keeps aside the disappointment. Your mind acquires mental strength by means of regular exercise you are made subject to. It is not always the favorable, but unfavorable circumstances too make you much stronger comparatively. Thus never be scared of the failures. Win over them with this determination in your mind that you are going to win.

*"Confidence building process of your mind would be depending upon the fact that what are the kinds of tools you have developed to maintain your confidence level intact? Understand that success is nothing but is an end product of failures provided you did not give up and stop from making efforts. Make it a conviction in your mind that although failures may come in your life journey but you are not made for failures. There should be no word like failure in your dictionary. So never fear failures."*

---

# 72

## YOUR OPTIMISTIC WILL

Whenever you take up any project in your life, you take it with the optimistic will to complete that successfully. Finally you find that you have done it. You have given the inputs of success to your mind cells so that there is conditioning of your mind to its sub-conscious levels. The functioning pattern of your mind would go so familiar with word success that it will start secreting chemical tools, generating to your capacity building, in the shape of your strong will power. Optimism is a mindset which exhibits its preparedness to stand against the odds, come what may. It is developed under the influence of friendly chemicals and continues to be stronger provided flow of such chemicals goes without break. There could be chances that you could not do it, the way you wanted to perform despite your mental preparedness. Never be over confident while taking any initiative in your life. Possibilities are always there either way. You could be the clear winner but at the same time you may lose it also, if you went overconfident.

Confidence is good but being over confident means you are going to develop a kind of tendency which would make you rash and negligent. You are negligent, means you are not taking proper due care and precautions to your initiatives. Therefore, possibilities of getting fail become much higher. This will cause harm to your optimistic will. How could you feel to be optimistic without applying to the law of action? Optimism being a state of mind, your mindset decides your determination and will power. You can shape your mindset with the help of conditioning of your mind. Have you ever experienced the factors which are responsible for enhancing the level of optimism within you? When you think negative, you will experience a decreased level of concentration of your mind. To be successful in your life and to achieve the life targets you need a concentrated mind for all the time. Positive set of mind strengthens your confidence level making you, thus more optimistic in your life. Optimism always reflects positive thinking in the sense that you start your venture with confidence that you will achieve the goal. Even if you happen to face failure for any reason, which is not within your control, it will not let you down with disappointment. Despite that you failed, you would feel full with positive energy to restart.

Feeling of disappointment is very harmful. You understand that this is a negative state of mind. No disappointment leads to your optimistic will. You have to handle this situation very patiently and carefully. Once this feel enters to your mind it takes to be a very tough task and loss of energy to drag it out. We are human beings and are prone to commit mistakes. But it does not mean that committing mistakes becomes a habit. Committing mistakes one after the other is going to make you weaker from inside. It would carry with it, loss of confidence and a trail of disappointments behind that. To whom are you going to make responsible for all that? Think over it for a moment. No doubt, we human beings have our own limitations. Alright, limitations taken but at the same time we shouldn't forget that we human beings have tremendous potential to perform and have done wonders in this universe. This became possible only because of the fact that we were optimistic that we can. Despite failures in the beginning but due to the optimistic will, we are able to reach the level of moon. Limitations apart, human capacities are wonderful which we are witnessing through progressive civilizations. This progress would be unending provided it is development oriented. But such development should not be at the cost of nature and be for welfare of the mankind.

*"Take your life with an optimistic will to succeed. Optimism always reflects performance with positivity. The input of success conditions your mind to its sub-conscious levels. Optimism is a mindset which exhibits its preparedness to stand against the odds, come what may. Optimism always reflects positive thinking. Human mind has a tremendous potential to perform, so is its will power."*

---

# 73

# WORLD PERSPECTIVES

You have unlimited scope for achievements in your life and sky is the limit for you, even beyond. At the same time this is also a truth that we have a limited span of life. In this limited life span we have to accomplish a number of novel tasks, which are not essentially for our individual benefit. When time is limited and you had to work more, then it is going to be a challenging a task for you to achieve all that unlimited, in a limited life span. The man has achieved unlimited to reach the surface of the moon and now planning to make townships over there. But to my calculations this is a simple and easy task once you are able to make up your visionary mind full with broader world perspectives. Develop your vision in a manner that your mind always thinks world class. Thinking world class will make you do things so that you are able reach up to that stage keeping the fact in mind that if you think average you will remain average. Let us not forget that our life has limited years with certain death at a particular point of time. For achievers of this world too, their life span has been limited but they reached on the top of the world since they had an attitude to exploit the unlimited scope existing around them.

One, having broader world perspectives, would not only need to think beyond human perceptions but he would also be supposed to perform equally world class. The powerful machine of your mind which possesses an extraordinary potential, would be instrumental in your pursuit to be the world class in making your initiatives of the highest order. Ground level is the stage which provides the base for genesis of your thoughts, whereas the middle level is going to be the stage of your journey when your thoughts are fully grown up and are ready to bear fruits. Then follows the highest level i.e. the top of journey of your thoughts with fruit bearing stage. Those who are able to enjoy the fruits would be beneficiaries of your endeavors. You will search around there your ultimate destination where journey of your thoughts reach to an end. In the process when your mind is flooded with ideas. It provides your ideas a fertile ground to grow up with. A positive thinking mind gives them healthy nourishment. Unless the grown up ideas get proper nutrition on regular intervals they die down undeveloped. We need to make an untiring effort not only to keep developing our ideas but to protect them as well from dying down. Nothing in this world is impossible for the human mind. Every human mind has an equal capacity to think and develop ideas. Sharpness of such capacity depends upon richness of thoughts provided that we work upon them consistently by utilizing the capacity of our mind.

Despite equal capacity, those who do not exercise with their mind, it becomes lazy and dull. You can imagine the sharp minds coming out with fertile ideas at the same time the minds which are quite blunt, either come out with no ideas or with dubious ideas. Thinking world class is much easier in the sense that there is less competition at the highest level and always there is space on the top. There would be full of opportunities once you are able to push yourself up from the crowd which is at the bottom and around the middle. The moment you are above and up the crowd, the sky is the limit for you and even 'beyond the sky limits'. This level in fact enables you to have unlimited scope in your life for your bigger achievements to rule this world. Let there be your life limited but your achievements would be unlimited since you have learnt to work upon your mind by thinking, developing ideas and applying them for the betterment of this world.

*"Always think big, world class, to develop your broader world perspectives with your novel tasks. Nothing in this world is impossible for the human mind. There would be full of opportunities once you are able to push yourself up from the crowd which is there at the bottom and in the middle. Always there is space on the top. Let the life have limited span but your achievements would be unlimited. Have the vision and work upon it to reach 'beyond the sky limits'."*

# 74

## UPS AND DOWNS IN LIFE

Ups and downs are regular features of human life. They come and go affecting life of the people. When it is up, people are happy with joy and happiness because they are successful. When it is down, people naturally are very sad because it is their failure. I have seen it very common that people go in depression while faced with diversities in their life. You should not be surprised by it. This happens with everybody. Diversities are quite natural in everybody's life. You feel certain happening to be diversity, if it troubles you. If such happening is favorable to you then you celebrate this as an event. Our life is full of ups and downs. It is not always necessary that things would go as per our expectations. I have discussed in my earlier chapters that we are just supposed to do our actions honestly, to the best of our efforts without expecting for fruits of our actions. There are happenings in our life which are no way related with our actions and are not within our control. Happenings caused by accidents are very painful but one cannot help it out except to extending consolations. We go in phases of depression and sorrow following accidents, loss of life and properties.

It is a psychological situation that people start expecting lot of things but at the same time they do not seem to be putting the needed efforts which are required to fulfill their expectations. Off course, the next question would be that expectations from whom? Obviously, you only. And who else...!!! You better understand as to how much efforts are required to be made to achieve the targets fixed by you? If you are failing in achieving your targets then please do not look for excuses here and there. Do not consider it to be any down stage of your life. You cannot make any plea that making sincere efforts were not within your control. Introspect within yourself as to where you went wrong and failed? And where did you lack in putting your efforts? If you are honest in your pursuits, you would be able to pin point your draw backs to improve upon them next and would be able to prepare the ground for your up stage. A series of ups and downs in your life take you towards the feeling that you are suffering from life adversities. Is it practically possible for a man to always get going for ups, without facing across downs? Is it going to be any way possible for one, to see the light of the day without passing across the dark phases of nights? Ups and downs follow up in our life are just natural phenomenon. If you are happy then you could be sad also at some stage of your life. Life is like this only as tempest, sometimes ups, sometimes downs. Take it as you like it. You just experience your own life journey. Did you never come across downs, while aiming for ups? Yes...!!! You would be honestly admitting this fact that it was all mixed with ups and downs. That is only the beauty of life. One would not be able to truly appreciate and enjoy the ups in his life unless he was able to boldly face the down phases of his life. By experiencing your failures to the core of your heart, you have earned your victory. You better understand the value of it and you have every reason to celebrate this occasion too. You were depressed the day you failed, the other day you were happy with success. But what you earned, you know that, it was not all of a sudden.

In true sense, these are the two dimensions of human life. Your life is nothing but a developing attitude of balancing mechanism between the ups and downs. The one, who succeeds in balancing the two, is the winner in long run. Developing balancing mechanism is nothing but is a psychological stage of your mind. Without getting depressed, face your downs and simultaneously keep making sincere efforts for your ups. A stage would come very soon that it goes in your habit handling beautifully with ups and downs. You are no more scared of it with a winner's attitude.

*"Our life is full of ups and downs. A series of ups and downs in your life take you towards the feeling that you are suffering from life adversities. Once you are able to develop a balancing mechanism between the two, you are no more scared of them. You will move with a winner's attitude."*

_____

# 75

## MASTER YOUR DESTINY

A man is the master of his own destiny. We make or unmake our destiny by the kind of honesty and sincerity we put in our efforts. Never think that it is anything of supernatural. Or it has to do something with your luck or fortune. There are thoughts prevalent in society that if luck would have it, you could have been successful in your endeavor. You failed because it was all bad luck. Luck based achievements must be discouraging for you. You may often hear people talking that he put all efforts to get that thing. Had it been in his destiny he would have succeeded? He felt sorry since the destiny did not favor him, he failed. They will say that it proved to be quite unfortunate for them otherwise no force on this earth could have stopped them in getting success. My plea is that we should discourage this tendency to connect our achievements subject to luck. This tendency of subjecting actions to fortunes makes people to sit idle, doing nothing and waiting for their luck to favor them, so that they are successful. It also becomes quite easier to throw all blame on to the luck for one's failures. People could be seen talking as they were not lucky so they failed. Making your struggles subject to a favorable destiny is apparently disappointing in my opinion. If one is keeping this perception in his mind then how come he is going to be the master of his own destiny? Come on...!!! Sit for a moment and think differently. Authentic winners are those who think differently and pave their own way to move on the path of success and glory. Whatever you achieved in your life was due to your hard work and not by luck and it was not as per chance. Yes...!!! That is true. Luck favors those who are sincere and brave by their heart and deeds. Never forget that you are destined to be the master of your destiny.

Man on this earth has made things possible which seemed to be impossible. Nothing is impossible for you to perform provided the matter is being handled by you with a determined mind. World scientists have reached on the surface of moon and are since planning to make colonies over there to settle down. Reaching on the moon has been a dream come true for the world space scientists. They made it destiny for themselves by putting in rigorous scientific endeavors for decades and decades and translating it into reality. The man made it possible, what appeared to be impossible to them at some point of time. Time space also has a decisive role to play in determining human destinies. Time is very strong. You need to put yourself in that time frame to decide upon your destiny and then establish that completely within that time frame. Give this thought to your mind that you are the master of your own destiny. There is a reason to believe in existence of natural forces which are going to frame your mind cells to make your destiny. The man cannot escape from his accountability to see that when and where in fact he went wrong? He must keep himself ready all the times to rectify his mistakes. He only is in a best position to indentify his faults whether done consciously or unconsciously. Please do not blame it on to human destiny, for the mistakes committed by people individually. Your destiny always keeps itself ready to favor you subject to the conditions that you keep yourself ready for favorable inputs to it. We are surely good with our destiny provided we act well and make others also feel good. Those who are resourcefully privileged, it could be but easier for them to master their destiny. But for the people underprivileged, for mastering their destiny, they would have to be dependent upon the mercy of privileged ones. This must be stopped.

*"A man is the master of his own destiny. Authentic winners are those who think differently and pave their way on to the path of success. Luck based achievements must be discouraging for you. It makes one to sit idle doing nothing and waiting for the luck to favor them to be successful. Man by putting his sincere efforts has made possible on this earth, the things which were impossible for them at one point of time. Time is very strong, move with it. Give this thought to your mind that you are the master of your destiny."*

---

# 76

## BE CAPABLE TO BE

Feel pity about such people who used to express doubts about your capabilities to do the things. It is in fact their malicious mind to keep underestimating you so that you are discouraged in your life pursuits. You will find people very rare who seriously and honestly appreciate your capabilities with all good intentions in their mind and they feel happy to see you progressing all the way. Appreciations of the people taken with all due respects but truly speaking you are the best judge to 'be capable to be'. The nature on this earth has made every person to be equally capable. This is the greatness and generosity of the nature that it never discriminates. Yes…!!! But the question arises then, why people on this earth are seen to be differently capable, under capable or even incapable? It is very good question indeed but not much difficult to answer. You cannot deny from this bitter truth that in the prevalent societal conditions people are denied from their basic needs even. Such system generated denials adversely affect individuals of their capability to perform. Societal conditions like poverty, malnutrition, poor health conditions, lack of proper educational facilities, no equality of opportunity, frustration among youth owing to unemployment and the governments doing nothing, are some of the prime factors responsible of system generated denials which affect capabilities.

Nature does not discriminate but manmade system discriminates. That is the real challenge we actually face all the time. But you have not to runaway away from these challenges. You have to be in the system and survive. Being in the system, you should not be discouraged by all these prevailing factors and system based discriminations. You do not wait for the negative people to give you any certificate of performance. You are capable even in adversities and hardships to perform well. In fact they are not capable to give you any certificate. You become stronger and more capable when you are denied opportunities. For a sensibly determined person like you, denied opportunities infuse strength. There are possibilities that you may be denied equality of opportunities by such people and you be deprived of from your lawful rights even. But it never means that you should lose your heart. How does it make any difference to you? They can at the most deny you any opportunity but they are incapable to deny your merits. There could be majority of people who are bent upon to put obstacles in your way of progress and prosperity. But you are capable, you know. You too, are a human being and not made up of any metal but your mind should be determined like a metal to deal with such situations.

Never doubt your capabilities and have trust in yourself. You should always keep in your mind that whatever the task has been given to you, feel confident that you are capable enough to complete that task. Nature has conferred you with equal mental capacity as compared to any other individual. Nobody can dare to stop you from working upon your potential to perform the best. What makes the difference as how you utilize your brain for your societal and material advancements in your life? Who are others to question your capability? It is not the grey matter of your brain but it is the frequency of the exercise you are putting in with your brain, your mind gets stronger and stronger making you more capable to perform. Subjecting your brain to exercises, no doubt is a strenuous job but unless you burn your midnight oil, how could you be capable to achieve your life objectives? Come on…!!! My friends. Be capable to be.

*"You are the best judge for you to 'be capable to be'. Negative people are nobody to certify your capabilities. Always have trust in yourself. Never doubt your capability to perform. There are possibilities that you may be denied equality of opportunities. But you have to survive in this system only. They can manipulate and deny you opportunities but they are not capable to deny your merits. You are capable even in adversities and hardships to perform well. Such denied opportunities make you much stronger and capable."*

# **77**

## FRIEND-THE BEST GIFTS

Your friends are the best gifts for you. The one, who has best friends in this world, is the happiest person on this earth. The human psychology behind gifts is that one keeps them very affectionately and carefully linked with its memories intact. Time and again he holds those gifts in his hands and gets emotionally charged. So the friends are, to be kept close to your heart, as best gifts in your life. Emotional bonding with friends is very strong and this basically is the reason that good friends are our strength. They will be your friends with whom you feel free to share the things which are quite personal to you. Friends are very caring and kind hearted. One should always be selective while making friends. A friend in your need is going to be your friend indeed. Let your friends not be much in number but they must be loyal to you. He will be loyal in the sense that under no circumstances your friend is going to ditch you in any manner or would cause any harm to you. You can prefer to restrict number depending upon your personal aptitude. Albert Einstein had been of the view that a man is in a position to utilize his potential to the maximum, when he is alone and is not disturbed and surrounded by undesired people. Amidst his friends the working potential of the person and his productivity of ideas would be enhanced like anything. It is absolutely for you to ensure that people who are not going to be anyway useful to you or who possess negative orientation should not be permitted to come close to you because they would ultimately harming you. And they are the undesired people as per the calculations of Albert Einstein.

Even if you prefer to be alone but this fact also equally holds good that you are for the society. There is a famous saying that man is a social animal. Social relationships with emotional human bonding are very significant. You also possess a human mind which needs sharing of ideas. Off course, sharing of ideas up to the level, your mind deserves to be. Making friends is a good habit but selectively. Good friends are assets in your life who are to be kept and maintained very carefully. What is significant is that how you are able to maintain your friendship and carry it on, to your mutual understanding and satisfaction? They are going to be the most valuable investments, your life can possess provided you are able to appreciate their value. Gifts in your day to day life are to be appreciated and kept close to your heart. They could be the most trusted people in your life with the association of whom you are going to climb up in your life, up to the sky limits and even beyond. You might have experienced that whenever you feel burdened with disappointment in your life, you always need good friends of yours, to be besides you. The moment you find that you are surrounded by your friends during your disappointments, the mental strength you gain is beyond expression. You feel protected then psychologically.

Your parents and the family members are closest amongst all. Behave with them friendly. Next come your friends who remained honestly associated with you in your life time. They are your gifts in the sense that they are with you when you need them most. They know you much better than any other person. They are ready to sacrifice for you. With your friends, you find yourself at liberty to share the situations of your life which disturb you, make you worry; they come out with solutions which would prove to be best possible in protecting your interests. Friendship is very delicate, handle it with care.

*"Good friends are your best gifts. Keep them close to your heart. Always be selective while making friends. It is true that a friend in need is a friend indeed. They are with you when you need them most. Friends are assets of your life in the sense that you feel at liberty with them to share the situations in your life which disturb you. They come out with solutions. They are going to be the most valuable investments your life can possess. Friendship is very delicate, handle it with care and preserve it."*

---

# 78

## FUTURE WILL BE YOURS

Can you say with complete certainty that future will be yours? There are sayings that why to think for future? So let us live in present, because living in present is good. But can we admit this fact honestly that while living in present, we never think for making our future? No…!!! Certainly not. It is human psychology that our mind, while living in present, always keeps wandering for a better future. But Yes…!!! Admitted one should not live in future, without making any sincere efforts while he is in present. Making desires for future and doing nothing to achieve it would prove to be harmful to you. Keep living in past is also not good since one has already lived up his life and the past has already gone. Do not forget your past mistakes because they give you an opportunity to identify your weaknesses so that you can rectify them and improve upon them. It will help you shape your future in a better manner since you will now take extra care to not to repeat your past mistakes.

Yes…!!! If you think, you can certainly make a statement that future is yours. Present is your time frame platform where you target for your future. If you are not able to strongly hold the ground today how could you be able to stand and move tomorrow? Your planning to move today becomes the foundation stone of your future journey. Keep in your mind the kinds of possible obstacles you may come across in your journey to your destination. Manmade obstacles in your way can not be completely ruled out. You perform in your present by always keeping your capacity to work in your mind. Thinking of doing beyond your capacity without making the required preparation for it is going to be very dangerous for you. Either you develop that capacity, which you can or think to achieve within your capacity, which you know, you can. The human mind knows the better way it could perform, the better it would be able to ensure its future. You would be able to say with complete certainty that you would have your future, for sure. You just think about the great leaders of this world. Great leaders were visionary and aware about their potential to think and work upon it. They also knew to enhance their working potential by practicing through perseverance. Individual apart they always looked for the situations keeping in mind the future of such civilizations, they lived in. With the future, intact in their mind they lived in present and did not forget their past.

How your past is going to shape your future? Nobody can claim to be perfect in the world. We commit mistakes consciously or unconsciously during the course of our performances. We do not claim ourselves to be super human beings. If we are alert then we are able to notice our mistakes and rectify them. Mistakes done with knowledge are going to adversely affect your career. Committing mistakes is quite normal but keep repeating mistakes carelessly are damaging for your future. Your sincere and honest preparation strengthens your work performance and to a higher extent reduces the probabilities of mistakes. Say then, with confidence that future will be yours. Great leaders of the world are able to do, what they decided to do. That should be the firm determination inside you. The great achievers are nothing more than any ordinary human being. But they are great learners, so they become great achievers in the world. You do practice it tirelessly. You would find that you have achieved your future life objective.

*"Making desires for future and doing nothing to achieve would prove to be harmful. Your mind while living in present*

*keeps wandering for a better future. Rectify your past mistakes and improve upon them. Repeating mistakes knowingly is dangerous. Great achievers of the world are the best learners from their past mistakes. Do not waste your energy for a thing, you cannot change. Your honest and sincere preparation strengthens your work performance and reduces probabilities of mistakes to a greater extent. Plan according to your capacity and get your future for sure."*

---

# 79

## EATING HABITS

You must be choosy while eating. Develop your well disciplined eating habits. Overeating is harmful. Eating in small quantities and at definite intervals is always good for health. To keep advancing in your life you need to have constantly good health. There is a famous saying 'health is wealth'. Once you have got human birth you have to achieve targets after targets with an avowed objective to serve the mankind on this earth. Keep thinking what is best for the mankind. Again that is going to be significant that a healthy body only keeps a healthy mind. Therefore, you cannot afford to be careless with regard to your food habits since it has a direct impact on wellness of your physical and mental health. You can notice that overeating makes you lazy and dull for the whole day. You will feel like sleepy all the time. While your profession demands an alert and concentrated mind, you are feeling sleepy. Is it going to work? Your boss is going to pass strictures against you. If your laziness is the reason behind incurring loss in production of your corporate house then you may lose your job even. For your excellent market value you are supposed to be an active and smart professional.

Your eating habits could be influenced by the environment you live in. The kind of company of people you are associating with, their eating habits are going to influence you. But still your good eating habits significantly do matter for your wellness and energetic health. If you are able to develop commanding position you will decide your food habits as to when and what you should eat? And how much should be the food intake for the whole day? You could be a person who likes vegetarian food or you could be non-vegetarian even depending upon geographical conditions. Your body needs definite percentage of nutritious components, viz. vitamins, proteins, carbohydrates, fats and other essential electrolytes in addition to water which is an essential component in your body. You might have experienced on number of times with your stomach upset following your bad food habits resulting in huge loss of water from your body. Essential electrolytes are also lost giving rise to your physical weakness for a longer duration.

Sugar is an important component for your body full with energy. This is useful for your health provided you are taking it in controlled quantities. But in modern times percentage of people is increasing regularly who are diagnosed with blood sugar. They become diabetic because they take sugar intake in excess quantities and without making physical exercise to burn the extra calories. In long run when medication fails to control then they are put on permanent insulin therapy. This is damaging for our health in as much as that diabetes is also responsible for malfunctioning of multiple organs of our body. We should not look for petty excuses here and there for this ailment. Our careless food habits are only responsible for such health problems. We need to strictly restrict our food habits within permissible limits of food intake.

Same is true in case of salt. Salt is also an essential component in our daily food. The moment you are careless about salt intake in your food you are going to be hypertensive with complaints of high blood pressure or hypotension with complaints of low blood pressure. Diseases relating to high blood pressure start adversely affecting your heart and malfunctioning of your kidneys too. Such adverse health conditions are going to hamper your professional growth relating to your life objectives. A minor carelessness in your eating habits can prove to be a serious health hazard in your life. You only can prevent such hazards by means of strictly regulating your eating habits. If you are non-vegetarian still green vegetables would be of much advantage for you. Eat less, live healthy. Live long with a fresh mind and active body all the time.

*"Overeating is harmful. Eating in small quantities and at definite intervals is always good for health. You know health is wealth. Your good eating habits keep your daily routines energetic. Your profession requires an alert and concentrated mind. Be an active and smart professional."*

---

# 80

## SETBACKS ARE BLESSINGS

Worries and setbacks are integral parts of the human life. Without them life is not complete. Your worries prove to be much painful compared to the hours of your happiness. Enjoy your happiness to the maximum extent. Human capacities are no doubt wonderful but are not unlimited. Do not make yourself worry for the things which you cannot change. While encountering with setbacks always believe in yourself that you can do that and turn your setbacks into your blessings of life. You will start feeling excited and full with confidence to move on. What the nature has endowed with in a person is not within his control. Nature goes by its own rule and regulations. It never discriminates between two individuals and strictly regulates them. We fall in setbacks when we do a thing which is not in accordance with the nature. Always keep this fact in your mind that everything is not going to happen exactly the way you want it to be because number of things is controlled by the law of nature.

We understand that we make sincere and honest efforts but we fail to achieve the targets of life. We go disheartened and worried if we face failures one after the other. Off course feeling of disappointment also goes by nature. Do we honestly analyze as to why we fail? Failures become much painful when our expectations go much higher. But this does not mean that we should not expect high. We need to put in the required level of hard work only to fulfill our higher expectations. Setbacks are welcome to rise again but to get worried about it is not going to be the remedy. Should we then consider that expectations are not natural? What would then be an expectation for success? It is quite natural that we expect to do and desire to get what we wish. Rare are the people who keep doing without any expectations. An expectation for desired result is co-terminus with the amount of efforts being put in honestly in that direction. We do lot many desires but we do not put in needed efforts to get those desires fulfilled. As a result of that we face setbacks. Let us admit this fact that we invited trouble for us. We need to seriously analyze the contributing factors behind our failures. Once we are able to identify them, it must be our serious priority to work upon them. There is no need to be worried about the setbacks. Let the setbacks come. They will come and leave you behind much stronger. Turn the setbacks into your blessings.

Clearly you have two options. You can choose to live up with setbacks of your life and become strong from within. At the same time you are equally free to surrender after being overshadowed by them. Choice is yours. You would be a weak person then. You must be surprised as to how come the setbacks are going to be blessings for you? Never forget that path of your final success passes through initial failures. Always remember that depending upon your efforts made, the success is going to be either momentary or it would be long lasting on permanent basis. The setbacks are the testing times in the life of every individual. Efforts to be made could be quite rigorous in nature. They could turn out to be blessings for you in the sense that you are enjoying adversities of your life with a smiling face. You never allow your mind to be burdened with setbacks. This you would not be able to do unless you work upon them with a confident and positive orientation. The day you started working with a mindset that you can do it, despite all setbacks, you are blessed to enjoy your setbacks. Work upon it, you would find that it works.

*"Worries and setbacks are the part and parcels of human life. While encountering with setbacks always believe in you. It is quite natural that we expect to do and desire to get what we wish. An expectation for desired results is co-terminus with the amount of efforts being put in honestly in that direction. The setbacks leave you behind much stronger. We need to analyze the contributory factors responsible for our failures and then work upon them sincerely. You will turn your setbacks into blessings. That is your strength."*

# 81

## ACT WISDOM

Wisdom is an inbuilt ornament of your personality. It reflects beautifully while you walk or you talk. At the time of taking decisions whether it happens to be a vital decision or ordinary, you apply the wisdom of your thinking mind. Well thought of decisions are very rare to get defeated. Your wisdom makes you to be a moving institution. It not only reflects in your words but it reflects in your personality as well. You do not speak a word but still it is reflected in your movement. The way you smile, the way you meet and talk with other people, it reveals the kind of wisdom you possess. Being wise involves the thinking process of your mind. There is a very famous old saying that you think twice before you take actions. This saying makes one cautious about decisions taken in haste must be avoided since chances are that they may bounce back. Before taking any decisions the wisdom always demands that we should look for the pros and cons of our decisions. Applying of our wisdom is going to bear fruits only under the circumstances when we apply our mind for those situations also which are significant in proper execution of our decisions so taken. Application of our wisdom would be of no meaning if the decisions failed to be enforced at the grass roots levels. To my understanding proper execution of our wisdom is more significant rather holding the wisdom simply. If your wisdom is for human welfare than the objective of human welfare should be achieved too. It would only be possible when you are applying your wisdom in defining the thinner rules of procedures necessary for its implementation.

Thinking process could be multidimensional. But most of the time it could be either thinking of positive thoughts or negative ones. Positive thinkers are the great motivators and wise personalities on this earth because they think wise, act positive and speak wisdom. The wisdom is nothing but understanding and doing different things in a rightful manner. Taking decisions which are beneficial to majority of the people relating to happiness in their life are of much vital significance. One should think what is just and fair, and is not prejudicial in any manner to the interest of the people at large. You are supposed to be progressive that's the wisdom of your life. Not only you, but the people who are in and around you, they are also accordingly oriented and are reasonably motivated by your progressive approach. That is in fact a very constructive achievement for you that your wisdom has created such an atmosphere among the people around you which would boost their personality multifold.

Why at all you should think badly for anybody? There could be people who may think badly for you. But still your wisdom lies in the fact that you are maintaining a kind of balance without being prejudiced against such people. You should have no time wasting for such petty thoughts. What should be the target in your life? Who would decide about it? Are you concerned with your personal interest only? What is wrong if the collective interests of the people are also included in your agenda? That would be a great thing. People are very rare on this earth that apply their wisdom and work in larger interest of the masses. The real beauty of your wisdom as a human being lies in the fact that you feel realize the sensitivity of your fellow human beings. You become restless as if what you could do for them? You need to make yourself to reach up to that platform, so that you could be in a position to do, what you intend to do for them. Yes…!!! You can. Are you targeting for happiness in your life, irrespective of the fact that you acted big or small? Do well for others. That's what you are wisely looking for. Act wisdom. Enjoy the beauty of life.

*"Your wisdom is inbuilt. It reflects in your personality while you move and you speak. Execution of wisdom is more significant rather holding it. Wisdom lies in understanding and doing, different things in a rightful manner. You are acting in a manner being without prejudiced even with the people who think badly for you. No matter. Act wisely."*

---

# 82

## PEOPLE THINKING NEGATIVELY

On number of occasions I keep talking with you all that thinking negatively is going to be harmful to you very painfully, sooner or later. Painfully in the sense that due to your negativity you are going to develop serious body ailments which are going to cause you pain. By the time when you happen to realize such life situations it would already go too late. My genuine concern in this direction would be to make my sincere efforts to motivate you all since beginning so that right steps are taken at the right moment of time when it is most needed to strike and be made a habit. Try to understand this in following manner. In due conformity with mathematical sciences take positive in terms of 'plus' and negative in terms of 'minus'. When you are thinking and behaving in a positive manner that is going to be an 'addition' to your personality and other achievements in your life. You are the gainer. While on the other side people who are thinking negatively that is going to be 'deduction' from their achievements and they would be the losers. People thinking negatively are full with negative energy. That negative energy in their body always reduces their capacity to work. This fact they are not able to realize unless they are able to completely control their negativity. This ultimately results into their poor physical and mental health leading to painful loss of their life.

If you minutely observe, you would find that negative thinking people are made up of typical mindset. They are not happy by their own wellness but they mostly remain unhappy for the wellness of the others. They start developing a kind of jealousy against them. There is a very important theory of elimination. If they cannot be positive then at least they should not be negative. No doubt, it is a tough task but it is not impossible. The elimination theory tells that if you are able to eliminate bad things, the good things are going to prevail inside you, very automatically without putting much extra efforts. The day you are able to eliminate negativity from within your mind, you will automatically become positive. There would now be enough space for positive and good thoughts in your mind. Negative thoughts are just like unwanted grasses and weeds which grow in our fields. Such weeds hamper the growth of our crops, so we need to remove them regularly from the fields to protect our crops. Negative thoughts are just like unwanted grasses and weeds. We would have to protect our positive thoughts by keep eliminating negative thoughts regularly from our mind. Let it be a slow process but it would be a certain process.

Negative thoughts cause much harm to the person himself who holds such thoughts, rather than the other person. May be temporarily they would be able to create problems to other persons and derive sadistic pleasure out of it. But at the same time they tend to forget that scientifically and biochemically their own negative action is going to have equal and opposite reaction, adversely affecting their body and mind. It is very easy to identify them as disappointed persons with disturbed peace of mind reflecting on their face and inbuilt in their personality. Such people have lost every hope in their life to do something for themselves and have developed tendency creating problems to others. They will show them as your well wishers and the moment they get an opportunity they will blow from behind your back. You are advised to identify such people from the lot around you. With a view to protect you from their negativity try to keep at distance from them.

*"People thinking negative are full with negative energy. The elimination theory tells that if you are able to eliminate bad things, goods things are going to prevail automatically. Negative thoughts are just like unwanted weeds and grasses in the fields which need to be removed at regular intervals to allow the crops grow healthy. Negative thoughts release negative energy resulting in poor physical and mental health of the individual. Eliminate negativity to allow access of positive thoughts in your mind."*

---

# 83

## THE WILL POWER

Your 'will' is going to be the ultimate 'power' in your life. You have been shown the way but you are lacking the needed will power to proceed in that direction then you would not be able to reach up to your destination. You wish to do things in your life but you feel weak from your inside and not able to take initial steps to start with. You will never be up to anywhere. For accomplishing anything in your life, whether big or small, you need to have will power. It could be depending whether how big your target is, accordingly strong will power would be the requirement. The famous saying is that 'where there is will there is way'. First of all what you are supposed to do is that to fix the target of your life. Merely fixing of the target only is not going to be sufficient for you. It needs sincere efforts to be put in those directions as follow up action. You would have to plan your way to reach up to your target. Simply planning your way again is not going to help you out unless you have the sufficient will power to pursue your target by proper executions the way you planned. You are not expected to pull your heart out right in the beginning itself but you are certainly advised to come out with such initial hits at least, so that it makes your intentions loud and clear that you are on to going for a big hit. It would not be necessary that in the very first attempt itself you are going to get your target but it would be enough to convey the message that you begun good with half done. That too, when your target has been full with competition from others and you survived. Never under estimate your competitors. They are also in the fray to compete with full preparations

Your target achievements are directly related with your happiness index. To live your life full with joy and happiness, carefully ensure that your will power is intact. Try to inculcate this in your habits that what you think you do. If you so feel that you do not have the capacity to do then better you do not think. You have developed yourself as a multi-dimensional personality, so challenges also are going to be equally big and of varied kind. On every front of your life you aspire to be successful. That is a great attitude which you need to keep intact. Your strong will shows you the way you have to proceed. Self-controlling your will power is very easy provided you have put yourself to a rigorous practice in this regard. Self-controlling would be a stage of self-motivation. The kind of motivation gives you the strength, you control yourself according to your plans you have drawn to reach the target. Your will power to accept challenges should not be influenced by any incentive given by others. Once your aspirations are made subject to such incentives then you would find that your will power is lost. This situation you should neither allow nor tolerate about it.

There should be no reason to repeat that an individual's will power is his state of mind. The strong your mind, the strong your will power would be. So the primary task would be to make your mind strong. This is completely up to you about the kinds of inputs you are putting in your mind, you are able to develop the self control of your will power. To strengthen your will power your mind needs a regular flow of positive thoughts. Not only such thoughts must keep flowing through your mental faculty but they should make your mind a permanent place to stay with. Once you are able to attain this position you would feel that you can now self-control your will power and can do whatever you would like to do and the way you desire the things to happen. Your strong will power would show you the way.

*"Where there is will there is way. You are not expected to pull your heart out right in the beginning but you are expected to have a strong will power to perform. Proper executions the way you planned would be the primary condition to translate the will power into reality. Self-controlling of your will power will self motivate you and would infuse in you the needed strength. For strengthening of the will power your mind needs a regular flow of positive thoughts."*

# 84

## BEHAVE YOUR SELF

Behaving is a basic human character. An individual is known by his behavior whether good or bad. He learns to behave under ideal family atmosphere by getting good training of behavioral patterns from his parents. He also imitates much of his behavior by living in the society, depending upon the kind of people he is associating frequently and regularly. Behaving under certain exceptional circumstances needs much self-control. Why behaving is significant in your life and for your future career as well, is a fundamental question? It is because of the fact that your personality is not one-dimensional but it is multi-dimensional. While pursuing your progress and achievements in your career you are going to come across with kind of people, who may prove to be quite helpful to you some way or the other. The most attractive dimension of personality is your social dimension. The way you present yourself in the society it matters a lot. You must be for social responsibilities subject to your capacity. May be you are not capable but at least you can behave. Your social behavior itself is going to contribute much towards strengthening the social bonds and establish social harmony.

Social dimensions of your personality are very beautiful. Your future career is going to be another dimension of your personality. Either you will get career opportunities in public sectors or private sectors or even you may have your own profession. Your behavior is going to be very significant for you in relation to your official output and your colleagues with whom you are working. No doubt, it is reciprocal and would be responsive with respect to the behavior of your colleagues towards you. But with a view to ensure that your official output is not adversely affected you should try to ignore their behavior and concentrate to complete your targets. You are required to be educated and knowledgeable too. You have to also support to majority of people in and around you who are ignorant due to lack of proper information. They are full of worries. It is their ignorance that they are not happy despite their well being. Your behavior would infuse soothing effect in them and they will develop positivity towards life. You will come across people who are not happy because they are incapable to fulfill their daily basic needs even. You must feel quite obliged to the Almighty that you are able to earn your livelihood without losing your self-control to your utmost satisfaction and also at the same time you are able to help them in their hours of need.

Behaving yourself literally means your individual perception about your own self. This perception is internally situated as an inbuilt feature of your personality. It is not the outer world but you are going to be the first person to keep an eye on your behavior and appreciate it first. Always respect yourself and move with self confidence. Your own appreciation is going to help you in improvement. You will mark that your feeling of self respect has completely influenced your behavior. You see others also with due respect. It is behaving in a manner that it all goes about giving respect to others and getting respect in return. You find that you do not demand respect but you command respect. The people who are in your company they also become equally sensitive and respectful. They are influenced by your behavioral transparency and honesty. This goes to be your strength which you earned by your consistent behavior. Amidst negative people you are required to maintain a cautious balancing in your behavior at the same time. Defeat such people by your constant honest behavior.

*"Behaving is a basic human character. An individual is known by his behavior whether good or bad. You should develop an individual perception and appreciation for your behavior. Self appreciation helps you in improving your behavior. You see others also with due respect. Always respect yourself and move with self confidence. People are moved by your behavioral transparency. Behave that you command respect and do not demand it. Defeat negative people by your constant honest behavior."*

---

# 85

## FAILURES STEPPING STONES

Nobody on this earth can say with full confidence that success for him is guaranteed on his very first attempt. There could be no doubt about it that persons achieved success in their very first attempt of career subject to the conditions that they worked hard, sincerely and honestly. That they did not leave behind any stone unturned to achieve the success in their maiden attempts. Such achievements are very rare. The credit must go to the person in individual that he established the precedent that success could be guaranteed provided you have worked hard. This goes to show without fail that where you could not succeed because you lacked in hard work, you failed. Again it should be noted that failures always do not mean that you did not work hard. But it needs to be pin pointed as to what was the factor behind it which contributed to your failure? Keep working hard. Hard work pays despite failures since your failures ultimately become stepping stones of your success.

The major factor which could be identified that lack of proper concentration of mind to your objectives leads to failures. If you are not concentrating to your work then your energy is not channelized in the particular direction of success. But at the same time your failures does not mean that you should go completely discouraged. Your life failures make you learn lot many things provided you are alert enough to note that at what point and when you went wrong. Never lose your heart even if you happen to face repeated failures in your life. You should not be discouraged by your failures because they are the moments of your life which are teaching lot many lessons to you. After taking those lessons seriously, you keep moving untiring, removing all the obstacles from the way of your success journey to reach up to your destination. Make your failures to be your success stepping stones. It should be your mindset that failures do not mean to be one step down but it should be one step up. Your one failure means you are one step up on path of your success subject to the conditions that you do not give up in the middle. Off course, it is agreed that it requires a lot of patience for a person to keep holding the ground tightly while he is in the middle, holding his breath for a while to keep moving on, till he is able to reach on the top. On occasions he may fall down feeling tired, going breathless but this does not mean for him that he failed. He knows that he possesses the winner's attitude and musters the courage to get up only to reach up to his destination. He could do it because failures could not deter him and meanwhile he was able to learn from his past mistakes and had also learnt to convert his failures into his stepping stones for success.

No doubt, failures are psychologically depressing making a kind of negative impact over the person. No one likes failure so it is depressing while nothing succeeds like success. Success makes everyone happy and full with joy. Apply your mind seriously. Keep continuing under depression for long would prove harmful to you. Then what are you going to do next, if you fail? Would you like to keep sitting depressed in a corner of your room with your fingers crossed? No…!!! You would never like to do that. You should never do it either. You will go sick by doing that and lose your all charm to work. You feel sad all the time and go lazy. Avoid this to happen to you. Think this way that failures in your life give you an opportunity for your self-realization and plug those loopholes which are adversely affecting you. Plugging your loopholes means you are getting stronger day by day. Meaning thereby the ratio of your wining and getting successful increasingly becomes higher than failures. Now you understand that you have made your failures to be the stepping stones of your success.

*"Avoid depressions arising out of failures. You feel sad all the time and go lazy. It is going to harm you. Think this way that failures in your life give you an opportunity for your self-assessment and plug those loopholes which are found to be adversely affecting you. Plugging your loopholes means you are getting stronger day by day and making your success stepping stones to keep moving on."*

---

# 86

## ENVIRONMENTALLY YOURS

How beautiful it appears to be when you are writing a letter to your loved one? You start depicting your love for nature by painting a rosy picture of scenic notes spread around you. Describing the beauty of nature in its entirety, the peace and spiritualistic pleasure close to the nature and the way you are enjoying the serene moments. You were able to experience the 'silence' through blowing winds across the dense forests. The day you noticed the flock of birds your window side as if they were inviting you to come and fly free round the sky. The clouds while entering inside your room and touching you nice cool. Your heart leaps up inside your body getting restless to come out and throw itself in the laps of the Mother Nature. You were not able to stop yourself and came out of your room in the balcony, you were lost for a while watching natural beauty for hours. You failed in expressing yourself through words. In the end of your lovely letter you are endorsing your love as 'environmentally yours'.

Imagine if something is being written to you by the nature itself and send to you in the form of a letter. Nature is virtual force on this universe. No one can deny with this fact. You will feel the force within you when the nature is going to endorse you in the end as 'naturally yours'. If you happen to go for searching history of the environment you will find the only truth that the nature existed before human civilizations got birth on this earth. What does it mean? It goes without saying that the nature and its environmental conditions were there to welcome your arrival and further existence as human being. Environmental conditions in and around you are going to provide you all that necessary protection for your survival. It would be much dependent upon the fact that whether to what extent you are responsive towards the protection being conferred by the nature? Your adaptability with the nature has been directly proportional to your healthy and joyful survival on this earth. Have you noticed that if you are gone sick? Means you have gone against the nature some way or the other. That is the reason for your sickness. Medicine would be of therapeutic importance only but unless you balance your metabolic and physiological conditions strictly in accordance with the rules of nature then make it a point, in long run medicines are not going to help you out. Go by the nature, you would find that your sickness goes and you are alright.

Nature has its own rules. It is a strict disciplinarian and keeps itself well within its regulatory framework. One should not dare to break the rules since he cannot survive by going against the nature. Our body has been endowed with natural capacity for adaptability in changing environmental conditions, so we survive and keep healthy. When you are not keeping good health, think as to where you went wrong against the nature? Changing climatic conditions in the environment are the rules of nature. Nature does give indicating signals to your body about its going sick. It is not all of a sudden unless some mischief has been played by you with your body. But we deliberately ignore our bodily signals and keep inviting troubles. If you are not keeping good health, you only are to be blamed. You need to go for a healthy and joyful life rather than a stretched sick life. You do not need medicines to be healthy and happy. Your body has its own bio-chemical mechanisms to your bodily resistance and to keeps you healthy full with your immunity power. No medicine can bring you the pleasure what you get from the nature. Happiness is not sold in the shopping malls. It lies with nature in abundance. Be with nature to be healthy and happy. Yes...!!! Environmentally yours.

*"You were able to experience the 'silence' through blowing winds across the dense forests. If we are not going by the rules of nature, medicines are not going to help us out in long run. Your body has its own bio-chemical mechanisms to your bodily resistance and to keep you healthy full with your immunity power. Happiness is not sold in the shopping malls. Be with the nature to be healthy and happy."*

# 87

## SPIRITUAL GREATNESS

Are you happy in your life? Do you think that your happiness makes you stay peaceful in your life? How does your happiness relate to your spiritualistic gain? May be you are happy and peaceful but that is only momentary. Make it a point that your happiness is nothing to do with your being spiritual. There is a lot of difference that 'you are happy' and that 'you remain happy'. Similar would be the situation when you 'go spiritual' and you 'being spiritual'. You are not able to say that you are happy in your life since you have number of liabilities to perform with. Can you anyway escape from your liabilities? You cannot. Then there should be no reason to be unhappy. You will be self-centric in case you are worried about your own happiness only. The day you have learnt to be happy in the happiness of others, this world is going to bow down before you for your spiritual greatness.

You can well understand the spiritual heights of such people who are worried about peace and happiness of others. They have crossed the limits of their individual levels of peace and happiness. There is a very touching story of a doctor. He was much dedicated to his profession for the cause of his patients. One day he was to attend to an operation of a patient in an emergency case. Every preparation for the operation was complete in the operation theatre. The paramedics and attendants of the patient were waiting for the doctor to reach, much anxiously. The patient was lying unconscious on the operation table. The doctor was getting late so the attendants were getting impatient and started losing their tamper. The paramedics kept silent as being helpless. In the meantime they saw that the doctor was coming almost running out of his car. The attendants started expressing dissatisfaction about his reaching late for operation. The doctor kept silent and without reacting to them, he went straight to the operation theatre. Got the theatre closed and started attending to the operation of the patient with full concentration of mind. It took more than an hour to complete the operation. The doctor after operating the patient came out of the operation theatre with a little smile on his face toward the attendants. He told them that the operation was successful and the paramedics would take post-operation care of the patient. And that there was nothing to worry about at all.

After saving the life of the patient, the doctor went straight to cremation ground to perform last rites of his son who died that day. Looking to situations at home the doctor could have either postponed that operation or he could have referred the patient to some other clinic in the city. But he preferred himself instead to operate the patient since he was well aware that the patient was quite serious. The doctor wanted to save the life of the patient as he knew that getting much late could have been risky for his life. The attendants of the patient who were critical about the doctor short while ago for his being late were shocked after hearing this news. Instead of attending to the cremation ceremony of his son first, the doctor preferred to attend to the patient who was critical. One could have very well understood the mental state of the doctor under the circumstances. But his strength and concentration of mind was wonderful and was the result of his honest dedication in the medical profession in the service of the mankind. Now they could realize the 'spiritual greatness' of the doctor in his commitment towards his patients when he did not hesitate to sacrifice his family interest and to save the life of the patient first. He did not think of postponing the operation under the mental pressure of his personal tragedy. This is the stage where the doctor has gone spiritual and has win over his worries to remain happy even in extreme adverse situations.

*"There is a lot of difference that 'you are happy' and that 'you remain happy'. Similar will be the situation where you have 'gone spiritual' and you 'being spiritual'. The day you have learnt to be happy in the happiness of others, this world is going to bow down before you for your 'spiritual greatness'. This greatness makes you win over your worries and remain happy even in extreme adverse conditions."*

———————————————————

# 88

## THE WORLD AWAITS YOU

You may be having a lot of personal works to perform. Many of them could be in your priority list. Professional requirements also need your personal attention on a regular basis. Looking to your business it could be very easily understood that you are not able to spare time. No doubt, that is quite obvious as to the common saying that 'charity begins at home'. Every person prefers to put his house in order first. It is for the well considered reasons that if one is not able to properly put his house in order then it would be very difficult for him to come out in the society and contribute accordingly. Let us not forget that as human beings we have certain social responsibilities also, as our moral obligations to perform. At the same time one needs to always keep this fact in his mind that the world is keeping an eye at you and it awaits you for the reasons of your sincerity and helping attitude to the needy. Not because that you would be doing something good for this world but also the world is looking anxiously to see you at the heights of glory and at the top of this world. You are different from others in the sense that you are not self-centered, so world is looking at you differently. Everybody does for himself and keeps thinking for his betterment. That is quite obvious too and being self-centric is not bad all the way but the one goes beyond it he scales the heights of glory.

You are different in the sense that you are seen expressing your concerns equally for welfare of others. However, you had all the choices to remain silent and mind your business. But instead, looking to the wrongs, you could not remain a silent spectator and you came out with your arguments for the wrongs to be undone. You have worked for them on your personal levels too, within your limited capacities, whenever such situations have arrived at. In today's social situations it has become a very difficult task to actually identify as to who is the well wisher of the people. People are cheated by foul players on several occasions, who are good actors presenting themselves to be well wishers for the rest of the world. They play malicious with psychology of persons and go for taking undue advantage of it. People of this world very innocently trust them to be, what they say to them. Winning over trust of the people by means of false representation of the facts is mischief and is highly objectionable. People feel stabbed from behind the back.

People of this world are so nice and innocent that they never doubt your credentials and take you by your face value. They do not see any reason to distrust you. Please do not say that it is their weakness. This is their attitude that they do not distrust you. Your responsibilities then go much high to emerge up to their expectations by keeping your words which made them to trust you. You then feel the kind of pleasure you are able to derive out of it. Clever are the people who go on exploiting their innocence. They in fact are the cheaters who betrayed their trust in a well planned manner. You need to protect such innocent people from dirty and malicious exploitation of such cheaters. What you only need to be an honest person. That's your real strength in them. People are very rare on this earth that is honest and trustworthy. You are one of them making your place in their hearts. Earning of trustworthiness is a very pious task. You know that you cannot betray their trust even in your wild dreams. People are in need of such persons and they are going to blindly trust you. Now it would be your strength to not to compromise with and sell away the innocence of such people. That would be painfully criminal. The world is awaiting you impatiently.

*"You are different from others so the world is looking at you differently. You do not remain a silent spectator for the wrongs done to people. You have your arguments to put forward for the wrongs so done, to be undone. People of this world are so innocent that they never doubt your credentials and take you by your face value. Earning of trust worthiness is a very pious task. Do not betray their trust in you. Clever are the people who go on exploiting their innocence. The world is awaiting you impatiently."*

# 89

## NOT TO LOSE TEMPER

Every individual possesses his own temper. It could be his 'good' temper or 'bad' temper depending upon his personal traits. But what is significant is that to be successful in your life, you need to maintain a healthy balance between the two. It is advisable that make such efforts so as to see that good temper is always on the higher side. You try to control and suppress your bad temper, whenever it happens to dominate over good temper. It is ordinarily seen that people avoid those who are known for their bad tempers. Your success depends as how do you behave with others? When you are a well behaved man, you are not going to lose friends. Do you feel yourself in the habit of being short tempered very often? Not only you are going to lose friends but you are inviting health issues for you as well. Not losing your temper indicates depth of your patience and the kind of mental stability you possess. What happens when you lose your temper? Notice that your heart beat has been increased. You start losing your self-control and feel that not able to speak properly. You are shouting at others unfairly because you lost your temper. Are you sure that by losing your temper you are able to get the work done exactly the way you wanted? If not, then what are you going to gain out of it? Nothing…!!! But your increased rate of blood pressure. Mind it. This is going to harm you.

You are amidst people who could be of average mental ability. It usually happens. Not all of them are of sharp minded. You have no other choice but to take work from them. They may not be able to respond to you as quickly to your patterns of working as possible. You are not getting expected performance from your staff for either they are average performers or they are not willing to perform. Getting disturbed is quite obvious since output has been reduced and your work is going to suffer. But you have no other alternative except to accommodate yourself under the prevailing situations. Possibilities are there that the people you are dependent upon have become a burden for you. Never hesitate then and instead of getting the burden over you, get rid of them who are not willing to perform. Those staffers who are honest and are willing to perform but they are failing due to their average ability; better train them to be good performers. You have to be very patiently taking work from them and simultaneously arranging for them good motivational sessions so that they are positively oriented. When you are able to develop a kind of healthy work culture with a strict maintenance of discipline including you, from top to bottom, then you would find that things would materialize as expected. It would also afford you all, with good learning environment for balancing of your tempers.

If you are a short tempered man then losing temper becomes your daily habit. Every other moment you are seen losing your temper for no authentic reasons. Losing your temper is not going to be a way out for getting the things done. Even when you happen to come across such situations that things are not getting done as per your expectations, you have to address them, with all cool and calm, to those people who are assigned with the said task to perform. May be in a one go or despite several efforts, they are not able to perform well, you may need to properly train them and make them learn their job. Be patient, they would be able to learn the things gradually. The reason behind social and economic backwardness of nations lies in the fact that people are not good learners due to its lethargic educational system. Your loosing temper on occasions could be justified but no way, go for a better stuff if situations so permit.

Not to lose your temper should be the message writ large on your face permanently.

*"Do not lose your temper. You need to make a balancing between 'good' temper and 'bad' temper. Not losing your temper indicates depth of your patience and the kind of mental stability you possess. Losing your temper is not going to be any way to increase your outputs. Feel the changes in you while you lose your temper. You are not able to self control and failing in to speak properly with increased heart beats."*

---

# 90

## GO FOR HELP

You must develop the habit of helping others. This is very significant human trait and other way round it helps in developing your personality in a positive manner. Think this deep as to how it is related with your inner personality? The feel to help others comes from your heart deep. A powerful sensation runs into your body and mind as a mark that you go to others with helping hand. People are great who understand the mind of others, who are in need of help. An emergent need for him could be a social or economic compulsion. Such compulsions come unwarranted. His needs are quite genuine one and honest. You are able to realize his honesty. Go and help him out. He would be the man who would not forget you through his entire life. You would then feel realize the kind of personality you are. You are going to help others and then forget about it all. You can then realize the moral strength inside your body and mind.

You must be experiencing all around you, today the world has become full of worries and very disappointing. People are not seen happy by heart. They keep running day and night almost for no gain, compared to the quantity of efforts they have put in. They have either no employment or are suffering from underemployment. A big majority of them lives in scarcities nationally and internationally. Such scarcities are due to social and economical imbalances prevalent in different corners of the world. State induced irregularities are highly responsible for all that imbalances. Those who are economically strong they rule the roost. The state made policies are also made to support them favorably. Worst sufferers are the poor weaker sections of the society. But who cares about? The governments do not look to be bothered to help them. People do have their own limitations to help others. But whenever any such exigency arises people come forward with open hearts. We should not forget that it is not individual but social responsibility. We need to develop tendencies to worry, not for individual interests only but for social interests too, as and when so required. There are well off people who take undue advantage of political machinery of the system but they overlook social interests. They do not help others. It is agreed that before extending help to others, one needs to see his capacity to help. Help not always in terms of money but many a times it is more emotional and psychological.

Any society is built strong by collective efforts of its members, means having tendency to help each other in times of scarcities. Everybody would like a society full with joy and pleasure. A person, who is in need of money to purchase his necessities, would not be happy. A person with empty stomach would not have the peace of mind. It could be easily seen that majority of people are disappointed in the society. They are poor, not properly educated and suffering from malnutrition and poor health. It is all for the reasons of defective state policies. System managers are not honest towards their state responsibilities. At the same time social system is also not that strong to come out with helping hands. This is absolutely unfair and unjust on part of any state. The state knows it fully well but still goes deliberate and careless since it has its own vested preferences, political and ideological. An individual has limited capacity to help others, going simultaneously with his family liabilities. He is great that despite all limitations he goes to helps others. Let us come forward united to make a campaign and force the state managers to ensure honest enforcement of its social welfare policies at the grass roots levels so that everyone becomes self-dependent. Happiness would prevail once our majority of people become so capable for their self-help.

*"The feel to help others comes from your heart deep. You must be experiencing all around that people are full with worries and disappointments. State induced irregularities are highly responsible for socio-economic imbalances giving rise to such disappointments. Happiness would prevail once our majority of people become so capable for their self-help."*

———————————————————

# 91

## AVOID OVERSLEEPING

Sleeping is good for your health. You need at least 7 to 8 hours of quality sleep. But keep sleeping for hours are not good. The needed sleep you take, it makes you cheerful, calm and active for the whole day. You might have noticed when you take sleep more than your body so needs, you start feeling lazy. Sleep and rest though associated with each other could be of two different dimensions. You did take sleep but still you feel to be restless. You could be restless either for the reasons of under sleeping or over sleeping. A balancing mechanism needs to be developed so that your sound sleep induces complete rest to your body and mind and you are able to perform well the next day. Despite the fact that you have taken complete rest, you do not feel like doing any work. Ultimately your entire day is wasted and your work production goes zero for the day. Keep sleeping is not only physical but you will notice when you are not alert, things around you also go like sleeping. Means no progress is found in your achievements. You do not find yourself in mental position to give well thought off instructions to your working staff. You notice no perfection and mistakes after mistakes are committed making mess of your entire activities. This would prove to be counter productive to your projects in hand. Therefore, you are supposed to be working with your watchful eyes.

You would have heard people saying that particular government or its officials are sleeping over the matter. It is an utter carelessness on part of such officials. Some way or the other, they deliberately delay the decision making process or absolutely no decision taken. This results in no execution thereby causing huge loss to the beneficiaries. Such situations on part of the governance are very critical. Careless 'sleepy' decisions make nations to suffer, not only socially but economically too. They consciously know that they are sleeping over the matter. They know that they are intentionally delaying the whole matter causing unnecessary loss to people who are intended to be the beneficiaries through such public policies. They do it not only because that it has become their habit but also for the reasons that it develops into corrupt tendencies in accepting some wrongful gain for them. Private sectors are very alert in the sense of their work performance since they do not allow their employees to keep sleeping over the projects and also for the reasons that this would be counter productive to them.

There is a term which is quite relevant in this regard. This is called 'sleeping sickness'. This term itself goes to explain that keep sleeping could amount to sickness patterns also. The people who are sick about sleeping, can never progress. It amounts to lack of action due to feelings of sickness. It has been noticed that there are people who have developed a kind of tendency to sleep with their eyes open. It could be a damaging tendency. In between tiresome working schedules ten-twenty minutes of naps could be advisable just to get relaxed for a while. Our literature, describe that those who keep sleeping are losers. At the same time those who are awake they gain. To be in action not only means that you are physically alert but you are mentally alert as well. Keeping healthy by reducing your excessive hours of sleep, would save your more fruitful hours which you can well utilize in productive work. Your achievements are going to be proportionately much higher with better perfection. One should always work with a mindset that his individual performances are going to be in ultimate interest of the society and the nation as well. Therefore, always work with this temperament. You would experience simultaneously that your nights are not restless and you are sleeping much sound only to get energetic for the day next.

*"Sleeping is good for your health but oversleeping is harmful. You take sleep but still you feel to be restless. Your performance is going to be dismal. In due course your disturbed sleeping schedule is going to be converted into sleeping sickness patterns. It will prove to be damaging not only for physical as well as mental health but would also be counter productive to your projects in hand."*

# 92

## HAVE MUTUAL TRUST

Human psychology is very significant in progress of civilizations and personality of the individual himself. Mutual trust and advancement of individuals always needs respecting others feelings. This component of human personality may appear to be quite simple but equally difficult to practice in our day to day behavior. It is going to be a very simple formula that if you wish that others should respect your feelings then the primary condition would be that first you should respect feelings of others, and then only you can expect others to give respect to your feelings. It is all about based upon the mutual relationships of give and take. There is a proverb which goes on saying that one should not demand respect but he should command respect. The basic consideration for commanding respect depends upon following factors. You must always remember that every person is sensitive towards his feelings.

Perception of self respect is the most significant personal character. Those who are careless about their self-respect could not be worthy of mutual trust. How could they be trusted upon that they would be serious about feelings of respecting others? Human feelings are not always bad but it depends upon how the other person acted first? If he acted well then the spontaneous reaction is going to be positively good. If action was influenced by bad considerations then the other person should keep ready for similar bad responses. It would be the greatness of the other person that he did not respond him bad despite the fact that his behavior was objectionable. This is the strength of his character which is open to be trusted upon. How are you able to protect your self-respect? It is a very valuable tenet within your personality. Once your self-respect is lost then make it a point that you are lost. Before you think that others should bother about protecting your self-respect, it is your individual responsibility to ensure that you are not going to compromise with your self-respect at any cost. Respecting others feelings has just an equal and opposite reaction. My observation to human behavior reveals that every human mind always responds in a positive manner, unless there are plausible reasons that it responded negatively. It also depends upon the environment in which such human mind has been groomed in. It could be an environment full with negativity, breeds only negativity. When in a given society there are disappointments all around, it's not expected people to be full with positivity. It is quite justifiable also under the circumstances, for which they should not be blamed for any such behavior, which is found to be objectionable. They would not have behaved that way knowingly but out of mere societal frustration.

By and large people are good and positive. They tend to mind their own business only. But due to unequal economic considerations, rich people do not respect the feelings of poor. Economic necessities of poor make them to be exploited at the hands of the rich. Our past civilizations have witnessed revolutions only to fight for respect. It was for respecting policies and off course, their hard labor. Same is also applicable in day to day life of every individual. Please...!!! Do not behave in a manner to any individual which goes on to hurt his feelings of self respect because he may respond to it, in similar negative manner. This may not be a welcome sign for you. May be one tend to, not to respect the feelings of others at the same time he is nobody to hurt him either? For your individual advancements in your life management initiatives, it would always be advisable that you respect the feelings of others then you experience the force of his positive response and the bond of mutual trust.

*"Mutual trust and advancement of individuals always needs respecting others feelings. Perception of self-respect is the most significant personal character. Self-respect must be your strength. By and large people are good and positive. Human feelings are not always bad but it depends as hoe the other person behaved first? Those who are careless about their self-respect could not be worthy of mutual trust. For a healthy society, mutual trust needs to be established."*

# 93

## UNDERSTANDING LIFE

Your life is very precious in the sense that you have got a human birth. We have to live up the human life up to its objectives for which we have taken birth. Understand your life, if you wish to live it and enjoy it. Enjoy your life because you are not going to get this life again. Do not waste it. For living up to the purposes behind our life we need to understand first about this life. Understanding life is very simple. In every body's life either there is happiness or worries. Looking to societal conditions there could be more worries and less happiness in life. There could be very rare people with more happiness in true sense and less worries. On occasions due to our bad habits, we make it complicated. We need to understand in its totality that what is the ultimate purpose of human life? We follow very common guiding principle that 'live and let other also live'. The moment we start deviating from this guiding principle, we start facing problems in our life. Your life has its own individual behavior depending upon your own initiatives like your approach towards life. Whether you practice positive things in your life or you are negative? These are the only two options. The only consideration behind the two options is that either you are welcome with happiness or you are inviting worries for yourself. Being positive means life is going to give you more opportunities to be happy and peaceful while the other way round, you should keep you ready to face the ultimate consequences. By understanding your life you will be able to grab these opportunities more accurately.

What we need to understand about our life is that we have certain goals of our life? If you either fail to set goals for your life or you may have goals but you fail to realize your life goals into reality then you have completely wasted your life. Do not befool yourself. That is criminal. Simply keep repenting is not going to help you out. Such goals are not only for your individual benefits but for larger social betterment too. Such goals you would be able to achieve only by keeping yourself happy, peaceful and content. If you get yourself disturbed then you won't be able to pursue, what you wish to do for yourself or for society. What makes you disturbed is your malicious thinking, in not letting others live. That is where you are going wrong in 'understanding life'. How can you expect to remain happy by doing wrongs and violating life principles? Make it a point, your life canvass is so big that even if you happen to fail in achieving your life objectives, your life keeps supporting you and gives you further more opportunities so that you succeed the next time. That is the inherent beauty of our life. Such life support is conditional provided you remain positive. Constant positivity for any individual is going to be a big challenge but can't help anyway. You have no way out but to practice that to continue with positivity if you wish to understand your life.

Being content with your life is absolutely in your hands. You have to be strict enough to ensure, to never allow any person to come close to you, whom you consider to be a man with negative credentials. You have to be very selective in this regard. Not only in case of people around you but to be very strict about the kind of thoughts which keep coming to your mind. It is a common human weakness but still we fail to take timely steps to win over such weakness. Your life is much accommodative when you face adverse situations in your life. Life intends to see you the winner. It is your life only which decides your high destinations and then keeps inspiring you to reach up to that. Once you are able to understand it, you are able to make your life more peaceful and full with joy and happiness. Love your life.

*"Your life is precious. Do not waste it. Understand your life if you wish to live it and enjoy it. Life accommodates and keeps supporting, when you face adversities and gives you further more opportunities so that you succeed the next time. That is the inherent beauty of our life. Your life inspires while it determines your high destinations to make you to reach up to that. Love your life."*

---

# 94

## ERROR IS TO HUMAN

We commit errors. Sometimes serious mistakes are committed by us, the human beings. The culpability of human errors are measured by virtue of the fact that as to what extent the human mind was in a position to understand that what he was going to commit was wrong? No doubt, this is true 'error is to human'. We all possess natural tendency to commit mistakes since we have no supernatural powers. Mistakes could be committed knowingly or unknowingly. The man committed errors in good faith and without any premeditation while he was executing his work honestly, by taking all due care and precautions. Mistakes could be excusable when are committed without any knowledge or malicious intention. But the mistakes committed with knowledge are culpable and not excusable. It is not very difficult to identify if a person has done mistakes deliberately. It must not be taken as excuse by way of making this a plea that 'error is to human', to justify our wrongs. It is often seen that people very casually commit mistakes and take this plea as defense. The caution is that we need to avoid it to make our habit for errors and then seeking excuses for being human.

Researches show that human mind ordinarily avoids committing mistakes unless there are deliberate attempts for doing any act or omissions. This is wrongful and we should not be deliberate in our actions. Looking to this natural tendency of mind, it is never deliberate on part of the human mind, to act upon in a manner which is not fair. It is just by virtue of some bonafide error, that some wrong has been committed to which the mind repents subsequently and it starts thinking to rectify the mistake. You might have honestly experienced in your life when you are feeling sorry for your errors and repenting to the extent to undo all that at an earliest opportunity. Your feeling about sorry for your error is indicative of this fact that you never intended to commit that error and it was just by mistake. Your mind is ready to accept that mistake, which should be the approach of life.

It is for the reasons of such bonafide only that errors of this nature are considered to be quite natural, as a part of human behavior. Mind does its work but errors do happen quite innocently since they too are inherent parts of human working patterns. Methods of trials and errors are very common. Mind would not stop from putting itself to 'trials' for the fears of inherent 'errors'. It is the part of the brain's function that it keeps trying for better achievements. In the middle it encounters with errors. It negotiates with such errors, removes them and moves further. Addressing to the errors is also equally significant since achievements are desired to be free from errors.

Problems in fact arise when it is noticed that errors instead of being incidental, they become intentional. People do commit mistakes with full knowledge to cause harm to others. Mind works in a positive manner but individuals deliberately influence it to commit errors leading towards culpable results. People then even do not repent for it. This is not, what is exactly expected from human beings to think in a manner, so that they could live up to their dignity. In the sense when human mind works under culpable influence then it does not confirm to the belief that 'error is to human', leading to degradations of morals as well, being more criminal. This needs to be strictly avoided by the people of this world. Errors committed intentionally are not in the protection and preservation of interests of the mankind.

*"Human mind works in a positive manner but individuals deliberately influence it to commit errors leading towards culpable results. Mistakes could be excusable when are committed without any knowledge or malicious intention. Human mind ordinarily avoids doing errors unless so done deliberately. Methods of 'trials' and 'errors' are very common. Mind would not stop from putting itself to 'trials', for the fears of inherent 'errors'. With all bonafide human brain keeps functioning for error free results and better achievements. Culpability does not deserve defense for human errors."*

---

# 95

## WIN OVER WORRIES

Your life is full of worries. One cannot just escape from worries but he has to manage them. Once you are down with worries then there would be a long spell of depression, you are going to face with. Phases of depression are not good for human health. They are going to affect your body and mind adversely. Once you are in with depression, now you are not a healthy man. It directly affects your mental capacity to work. You keep feeling lazy. Do not like to work or enjoy and feel disturbed all the time. Down under depression means you need to activate your mind. You would feel that you have gone dull. You do not feel good. You are not happy in the sense that you are overpowered by your day to day worries. Once worries strike at you the only two options you are left behind. One option is to either live with your worries or the second option is to get rid of them. Living with your worries would not be a solution and would be harmful to you since further more worries would be in waiting to trouble you further. It will then prove to be an endless trail of tragedy for you and not advisable. The only best option left behind is that to get rid of your worries. Human mind has the capacity to train itself in such a manner that it could face worries and win over them provided you are coming forward to fight with your worries by holding and pushing them head on.

We need to think upon as to how come worries trouble us? And how come worries are able to overpower us? We should very honestly admit this fact that we invite worries for us. We allow and give them the space to enter into our mind and then allow them to stay there. The natural worries like death of any beloved one, sufferings from sickness, accident etc. are quite incidental, which are not self-induced. Such incidental worries are not within your control. You feel sick because of negative thoughts inside you. Who permitted the entry of negative thoughts to your mind? It is just like, you carelessly allowed entry of viruses in your computer and which goes corrupt. Now you are giving it the doses of anti-viruses to clean your computer system so that it is back in its shape. This is your problem of worry which you allowed to happen. Had you strictly controlled the viruses of negativity to your mind, you would have definitely avoided falling sick. The anti-viruses to your worries are your positive thoughts, self-confidence and your determined mind. This way you could have won over your worries.

But what to do once you are down with worries? Since majority of us are responsible for our own worries, therefore solutions lies with us only. We have created the problems so we have the solutions provided we are strictly adopting those solutions in our life. You would also agree to it that practicing positivity is the only effective remedy to counter negativity. It is no doubt a tough practice but once you are able to achieve that it is going to last forever with you. System generated societal situations are also potential causes of social worries of serious nature which are again not within the control of an individual. These are not the worries which could be self-induced but it is due to serious system failures at the levels of socio-political governance. This becomes a matter of grave concern for our existing civilizations where day-to-day fulfillment of basic minimum requirements has been linked with economics. The poor economies are bound to be down under varieties of sufferings and worries. This becomes a very unfortunate situation, where poor are absolutely unable to win over their worries unless the governmental mechanism supports them honestly.

*"Once worries strike, the only two options with you are either to live with your worries and spoil yourself, or make efforts to get rid of them. Admit honestly we invite worries by allowing negative thoughts to enter our mind and go sick. It's just like allowing viruses to your computer and it goes corrupt. You need anti-viruses to bring your computer system back in shape. Negative thoughts are viruses to human mind. Treat them with anti-virus by flow of positive thoughts and get rid of your worries."*

# 96

## RELIGION TO BE HUMAN

We in human civilizations go for a society which behaves in a manner which is not unbecoming of a human being. Religions on this earth have been linked with human conduct. Human beings should conduct themselves strictly according to their birth as being human. Religion could be defined in very simple words. It is nothing but codes of human conduct so that humanity survives on this earth. Regards origin, human came first on this earth then came religions. Being human or practicing humanity is the best religion one can adopt in his conduct. People think and behave in a manner which is for the betterment of the mankind on this earth. Not only for the mankind but they should behave human like with animals too. There are different religious beliefs which are existing on this earth. There are communities which have faith in such religions so they are the followers of such religions. So the religion survives provided it has kept its followers intact. It could be understood as 'religion is to human' or vice versa 'human is to religion'. One religion may have its strong foothold among its followers in a particular region at a particular point of time, while it may lose its ground at a different point of time. When religion is the moral code of human conduct then it could be very safely concluded that all religions reach to the same destination for human good and feeling of brotherhood.

Every religion with its distinct origin has the same destination of human welfare. Why then we come across conflicts based upon religious considerations and contradictions? It is a big question of serious concern that instead of spreading feel of human welfare and peace through different religions, there are reported instances of spreading religion based hatred among different religious communities. This becomes a very painful situation for us being human with differences. Once such hatred creeps in the minds of such communities, it goes very difficult that communities live in peace. No religion on this earth goes for any kind of feel of hatred among human beings. The burning question is that who are the people responsible for spreading feeling of communal hatred? Religions do not do so. All religious teachings go for love and peace. Then it could be said very safely that there are certain elements in different communities who in the name of being followers of such religions, break their codes of human conduct causing communal disharmony among people. This needs to be stopped by the religious leaders, if they happen to claim having their control among the followers. If not, then it is going to be too late. A person believes in humanism by practicing humanity among human beings. His plea is that he believes what he sees through his bare eyes. If he is able to feed a man who is hungry then he feels that he has served the humanity and that is his religion. One is spending exorbitantly but is not spending a single penny for a needy person; he is not a religious man.

It is very clearly being noticed that political leaderships also exploit religious differences for their partisan political gains. They do not have any bonafide to seriously think about it and do something for resolving such differences, so that there is lasting peace and brotherhood. Such tendency is going to prove to be very dangerous. Religion is to be human. Human relationships are meant to be for mutual brotherhood and happiness. Different religious faiths prevalent on this earth are to strengthen the bonds of human relationships irrespective of their caste and creed. The religions are to protect human sentiments and make such mechanism that there is no such conflict of human interests which is going to impact breach of peace. Let us go for religions which are for humanity and mankind.

*"Religion is to human, or human is to religion. All religions on this earth reach to the same destination of human brotherhood. Instead of spreading peace, spread of communal hatred, is disappointing. All religions go for mutual love, peace and brotherhood. No religion goes for spreading hatred between communities. Religion is to be human. Let us go for practicing humanity on this earth."*

---

# 97

## PARENTS REAL GODS

You owe your existence on this earth to your parents. They gave you birth on this earth and you grew young under their sentimentally vigilant care and protection. Under proper care of your parents, you not only started learning this vast world but you also learnt how to survive in this unpredictable world. Imagine when you were infant and crying out of your innocence, your parents were there to hug you in their laps and gradually to bring you from darkness to the world of knowledge. To make you know that your life is full with beauty. Make your life worth it and enjoy it. You remember that when you went to school your mother did not take meals till you are back. While your father used to miss your lovely company since he had to go out to earn the livelihood for the family. You had your other brothers and sisters, your parents had to look after them. They maintained a balance so that you all grew well to face the challenges of your life. In scarcities they slept without food but they were not ready to see you hungry. When you used to be sick in your childhood they had restless and sleepless nights caring you to make you cure. You have not seen them weeping in their hardships but they used to weep by their hearts so that you are not sad. Your parents sacrificed their all interests for the sake of your well being. They ensured that at any cost you are not put to at any hardship in your life.

Time is never static. It keeps moving fast and that is the beauty of time. By your youth you were engaged in your job. It was not necessary that you were going to get a job so that you can live with your parents. You may get a job away from your parents. A stage comes when your parents become aged with the passage of time. It is said that old age is just like childhood. There is no much difference between a child and a old man. Then they need your physical and mental support to the maximum. This support is because they still had the same childhood caring for you. You sometime become so busy in your work that you are not able to find time to spend with your parents. This parents well understand that you are occupied with your work. They like your business and always wish the best for you. They do not expect that you should break your busy schedule for them. Their happiness lies in the fact that you are happy. They go very sad when they see you disturbed and worried. It is also found that on occasions parents are ignored deliberately. Make it a point in your mind that if you are ignoring them but still they will wish the best for you. The parents are the real Gods on this earth. They never expect from you anything in return for what they did for you when you were a child and growing young. Here lies the greatness that they always desire to keep doing for you all through their life despite the fact that they grow older and weaker.

What can you do for your parents? Do you think that you need to plan, to do something for your parents? If you feel to make a plan for your parents then make it a point that you are ignoring your parents. There could be no separate plan for well being of your parents. It goes side by your plan. You cannot be that formal for them. It must be in your daily routine that you are properly taking care of your parents. You worship Gods that is your religious consideration. That could be just symbolic. But your parents are the real Gods, in front of you, on this earth. Worship them with the core of your heart. You see in them the real Gods. You love them as real Gods. You can feel them that they are with you showering all love and affection to you. You feel then that you are the happiest person on this earth.

*"We owe our existence on this earth to our parents. Your parents sacrificed all their interests for the sake of your well being. They are happiest when they see you happy the most. They are worried and go restless and sleepless, when they see you sad. They never expect from you anything in return, for what they did for you when you were growing young. Worship your parents as they are the real Gods, in front of you, on this earth. You see in them the real Gods. You love them as real Gods."*

_____

# 98

## STRUGGLE HONESTLY

Life is struggle particularly for those who are not born with a silver spoon in their mouth. It is not within control of anybody that he will take birth in a family of his choice. May be you are born in a family which is not well off. It will not be said that you are born with a silver spoon in your mouth. But still you have a feel of proud in the family you are born. You understand that your parents struggled for you to support your existence so you will struggle now for your parents and their well being. In whatever fields of life you want to be, you need to struggle honestly. You desire the glory and respect in your life then your life struggle with honesty would be the primary condition. How you are going to define your struggle? You are making untiring efforts to achieve the goals of your life. You get your goals well in time or may be you fail to achieve despite sincere efforts. At the same time you come across number of obstacles in your way of life. Such obstacles could be either natural or are manipulated in your way by your opponents maliciously to deter you from your path of success. You may be struggling quite honestly but still you feel denied from the fruits of your struggle. It frustrates you, which is quite natural. You are also a person having with all kinds of human sensibilities. You too feel hurt and depressed when you find that things do not go the way you struggled for.

No doubt, scarcities in one's life are going to hamper his struggling pursuits but still despite scarcities one should optimistically enjoy his life struggles. One cannot expect struggles without obstacles. Keep yourself mentally prepared for situations which are also called as adversities of life. Natural obstacles in your way are understood and you are already prepared for them, but manmade manipulations in your way are very dangerous. You neither expected nor were you mentally prepared for it. Your struggle becomes more rigorous and painful when there are people after you with all negative orientation to pull you down. Never bother for them. What you need to do, is to identify them and keep alert before they succeed in harming you. No doubt your struggle goes quite tough against such polluted and malicious minds but at the same time it makes you much stronger from within. You develop your mindset in such a manner that you exploit such adverse circumstances to your advantage. Sailing against the winds is quite troublesome but once you have developed the needed skill, you are unstoppable then. You keep struggling and never allow such malicious minds to come close to you. Because being close to you would be quite convenient for them to put obstacles to you and harm you.

Even otherwise also your struggle must be honest. Honest strugglers are the perfect strugglers with their confidence level and body language intact writ large on their face. Do not struggle just for the sake of struggling and to show others that you are struggling as such. You are not struggling for others but for yourself. It is your inner conscience which authenticates your moves that you are putting in your efforts into a right direction. Your mind knows well whether your struggle is just formal or is serious in nature. With full determination, once you are honest to yourself, and moving towards your goal, nothing on this earth can stop you from getting successful the way you wanted. Always self-evaluate your efforts on path of your struggle and that would be the best feedback for you in your struggle and to reach on the top of the world.

*"May be you are not born with silver spoon in your mouth. You feel proud in the family you are born. Your parents struggled for you and you are struggling for your parents. You are making untiring efforts to achieve the goals of your life. Sailing against the winds is quite troublesome but once you have developed the needed skill, you are unstoppable then. Honest strugglers are the perfect strugglers with their confidence level and body language intact and writ large on their face. Always self-evaluate your efforts and keep moving on the path of struggle till you succeed."*

---

# 99

## NO SECOND INNINGS

This is very bitter and bare truth of our life that we have got only one innings of our life. There are no second innings of our life. Always do well in your this innings of life so that there is no occasion for you to repent in your life. You must be having your well defined life objectives and well drafted action plans. To achieve your life goals the primary condition is that your action plans need to be nicely executed in their true letters and spirits. You cannot afford to keep postponing the execution of the action plans of your life. The execution of your plans is to be completed within a defined limited time frame only since the life has no second innings. Make your life beautiful and of others too. You are not going to meet them again or wait for them even. When your life innings are completed and you are getting ready to leave this world there would be no chance for you to repent even. In this innings it is you only who will make your life a memorable event. You have to manage your life activities in such a manner that you achieve your life objectives to the maximum and make your life beautiful. In your present span of life you have to do all the good deeds so that you feel satisfied in yourself that you lived your life with complete justifications. You cannot risk to keep pending your targets, just under the impressions of your first innings and then to think about to complete the leftovers nicely in the second innings. People may believe in rebirth, but to those who go for logics and reasons there is nothing like rebirth or second birth of a person. Therefore, you have only one life span for you and see that it is not wasted.

Life is for love and affection to each other. This must be the fundamental goal in anybody's life. In a beautiful life we are expected to play beautifully, the only innings of our life we have. We came in this world with a sense of pride so we should leave this world too, with a sense of same pride or even more. Do not let the people cry when you are going to die. They are going to remember you with their eyes full with tears and your memories intact in their heart deep. Let a sense of brotherhood to prevail with each other. You may be having your own work plan for yourself and your family. You equally look concerned to do something for the society as well. Honestly speaking, it is not going to be an easy task to nicely balance between family interest and social interest. Charity begins at home so, no doubt, take your family first but do not forget the society in which you live. You are not going to get this life again. You have got only innings to perform as well as you can.

If your first innings has gone waste so you feel, you repent for an opportunity to do good deeds in the second innings. Had there been a second innings of your life you would have done a lot. But you know that you do not have any second innings. So you are repenting useless as your time is gone. Make your life worth living by your positive deeds so that you die with peace. By doing all negative deeds in his life, now the man repents in the last leg of his life, when he is about to die now. Let somebody tell him that no one can help him now? He could not live in peace, let him be die in peace. But nothing could be done since life innings are completed now. Everything is gone; others are also just waiting hopelessly. Now no opportunity to convert your bad deeds into good ones. Death is the ultimate truth of your life. You cannot escape from it. On your death bed you remember your bad deeds. But it would be of no use. You have wasted your whole life, now you realize. Your good deeds would have been there to help you to die with peace. Death without peace is quite painful. Ensure that you die with peace and happiness. It is possible only when you are honest with your deeds in your only life time.

*"There are no second innings of your life. Life is for love and affection to each other. Do not let people cry when you are going to leave this world. People would see you off from this world, with their wet eyes and your memories intact heart deep. Your good life deeds would help you to die with peace. The man could not live with peace, let him be die in peace."*

---

# 100

## SKY IS THE LIMIT

Those who wish to fly high sky is not the limit for them. They intend to fly with a vision even 'beyond the sky limits'. Yes…!!! You have the capacity to go beyond the limits of sky provided you have the determination to reach up to the sky. Once you have scaled the sky limits then you are getting a space unlimited and you are unstoppable. While it would depend upon individual efforts of the person, not everybody reaches up to the sky. I mean to say that as you reach the sky limits, competition would be much less up there and you would be able to make your space on to the top. The sky is unlimited so are your ambitions. Take it this way that sky is the symbolic motivation for you and it keeps inspiring you to fly high in the sky. When you would see from up the sky, you will realize this fact that how small the world has become for you? For your achievements it is always said that you keep performing, sky is the limit for you. Scaling the unlimited sky is made possible by our space scientists while they are preparing to settle down by establishing colonies on the moon surface. The limits of sky motivate us. If one is able to maintain his courage intact, he can make things possible which otherwise may appear to be impossible. Once you have set your target that you have to scale and reach up to sky then one after the other, your achievements are also going to be unlimited. You set your targets by applying to the thinking process of your mind. So you have to scale the sky, then you sit and apply your mind and think about it. Thinking process cannot be limited one, it must be world class. It may take years and decades of making work plans and keep implementing. You think, you can, and you win.

You are targeting to reach up to the sky. You may not be able to scale the sky limits in one go. Your failures in the beginning are going to be the stepping foundation stones of your success. Failures are going to put you under worries. But you are up, not to give up at all. That is going to be your real strength in never to give up attitude. You would need to keep making efforts optimistically without looking back. There could be obstacles on your way while scaling for success. You also understand that measuring the sky limits would not be an easy task. So you are approaching with this frame of mind, which makes sure that your failures are not going to deter you in any manner. They are not able to cause any trace of fear in your mind. You are going to define your destiny and you will be the master of your destiny. You may come across series of failures also while pursuing your goals but that would be your testing times in real sense. Just watch a small spider while it is knitting its web. In the beginning of it, the spider makes number of failed attempts to ride on the wall and to reach up to the height of the corner of wall. Knitting of the web for that small spider was not complete in a one go. While knitting, the spider used to fall down on the ground innumerably but every time it starts scaling the wall afresh reaching on to the wall corner only to fall down again. But it did not stop till it successfully knit the web. We need to take big motivation from the small spider that you are made to win. Never give up. Keep making untiring efforts till you reach 'beyond the sky limits'. You should come out with your projects in your mind with full determination and confidence. The world will see that you are going unstoppable, successes after successes, and achievements unlimited. After all sky is the limit for you. No...!!! One day your mindset would be so formatted with success that you will start thinking in terms of 'beyond the sky limits'. You will do and you will make others also, do it up to the sky limits and even beyond.

*"The limits of sky motivate us. You think, you can, and you win. Learn from the small spider knitting its web by falling down innumerably but still scaling the wall finally. You should come out with your project in your mind with full determination and confidence. While scaling the sky limits, you are unstoppable, formatting your mindset to think even 'beyond the sky limits'."*

───────────────────────

# 101

## THE CORONA WARRIORS

Since beginning of the year 2020 the entire globe is witnessing the outbreak of novel corona virus, which has spread about in more than 156 countries in the form of pandemic. No vaccine has yet been discovered by our world scientists to cure this disease. However, they are engaged in their research day and night to come out with a vaccine to fight this novel corona virus out. There has been an old saying that 'prevention is better than cure'. Now under the circumstances when there is no cure, yet then prevention would only be the best option. The world countries are going through unprecedented phases of lockdowns so as to counter the spread of pandemic. It is unfortunate that people are dying painful deaths. Salute to our 'corona warriors' that by putting them very close to the risk of deadly corona virus they are trying to save the life of people on this earth. By getting exposed to all risks of viral infection to them, they have put their lives in dangers. They are able to attend to their humanitarian duties only on the strength of their strong will power and their commitment in the service of the mankind.

Let us trace the background of this novel virus converting itself into pandemic world over today. The corona virus disease 2019 (Covid-19) has been reported to be a fatal illness caused by a novel corona virus all across the globe. It has been named as severe acute respiratory syndrome corona virus 2 (SARS-Cov-2). This was first identified during outbreaks of respiratory illness cases in Wuhan City, Hubei Province of China. On 31 December 2019, the Wuhan Municipal Health Commission came with reports of a cluster of 27 pneumonia cases with unknown etiology. All the cases had common reported links with the wholesale fish and live animal wet markets at Wuhan. On 09 January 2020, China reported the novel corona virus as causative agent behind pneumonia cases. On 30 January 2020, the World Health Organization declares this first outbreak of novel corona virus as 'a public health emergency of international concern' and on 11 March 2020, it was declared to be a 'global pandemic'. Since 31 December 2019 and as on 01, June 2020, in total more than 63lacs cases are reported to be positive with novel corona viruses and more than 04lacs deaths reported all over the world.

Let me argue with my humble submissions in favor of natural conditions for protection and preservation of our environment. We have already done a lot of harm to the nature in the name of development, which is not for all but for those only who could afford the benefits of such development. It would not be out of place to mention that the blind race of rich developed countries has ruined the ecological balance of flora and fauna. Biodiversity on this earth is right now in crisis, or rather we should admit it this way that the earth itself is going through crisis because of disturbed biodiversity by us. The air we breathe, the food we take, the water we drink and for variety of life on this earth, we rely upon a biodiversity. Biological diversity has its own balancing mechanism to sustainably preserve the environment and without it survival of humanity is not possible on this earth. Extreme global warming and cooling has become order of the day. Unpredictable climate change conditions have become surprising even to the experts. This must go on record that such frequent ups and downs in climatic conditions goes on to adversely damage the immunity mechanisms of human body system. Mother Nature is to protect us the humanity with all its balancing mechanisms in the form of its ecosystem. But our greed has made us run amok exploiting the nature to the brink of its destruction. The world leaders developed a kind of fanatic belief that by exploiting the environment the way they like, they are going to win over it and rule the nature. But the nature has its own laws to control and regulate this universe. They completely tend to forget that this world is at the disposal of nature and not the vice versa. The nature on occasions gave honest signals to us in the form of natural disasters that enough is enough but the world remained criminally ignorant. Now the world with no clues of any kind, is helplessly fighting the worst ever disaster in the known history of human civilizations. We, so painfully and miserably, are in our desperate bid today, attempting to balance on the brink of possible collapse. The outbreak of Covid-19 on such a large scale all across the world goes to establish its links with disturbed biodiversity owing to its origin from Wuhan wet markets in China. While experts researches are in progress but possibilities of this cannot be ruled out.

The entire world is witnessing the doctors, nursing staff and paramedics in the hospitals have become the Gods while rendering all possible medical care to the victims of this novel corona. It's a scientific fact that this virus spreads man to man, but still undeterred by all that, these warriors are attending to their patients fearlessly. They have sacrificed their own family interests, leaving behind their kids and quarantined them in hospitals day and night so that they are able to perform their pious work of saving the life of corona patients. Looking to the quantum of reported deaths world over till date, one can very easily understand the deadly nature of this disease. There are ample numbers of recovery cases also with all credits to the health care warriors. The sanitary staffs of respective city municipal corporations are the warriors, next in the chain, who contributed by means of sanitation and cleanliness processes which are essential in proper maintenance of health and hygiene, particularly in the wake of current pandemic.

The police personnel as warriors had to fight a very tough battle in strictly enforcing and regulating lockdown restrictions. Red zone hot spots were the very sensitive areas for containing spread of the virus to safer zones. Restricting inside their homes, with no outside movements, that too for months and months altogether, had been unprecedented as never before, for currents generations. Obviously, lockdown violations were bound to take place since liberty conscious people were fed up by these restrictions, which were hampering their freedom of movements. Number of protests by supporters of personal liberty and freedom of movement were reported from different corners of the world. But the police had its own priorities on cards in containing the spread of corona virus and strictly keeping the protestors back in their homes.

I consider the poor labor communities from weaker sections of the society, also among the corona warriors. All of a sudden this community was locked down, left with no choice. The factories, industries in the commercial sectors were shut down with immediate effect. The labor community was left unemployed. With all transportation facilities completely shut, they were not able to come back to their homes and were held up for no reasons. They could have well been transported right in the beginning itself but due to defective decision making at the highest levels, labor communities were made worst sufferers of corona lockdowns. Horrible...!!! Males and female workers started walking down back to their homes through roads and railway tracks, some thousand miles away from their workplace, with their kids in their laps and their belongings on their head. Number of them sacrificed their life while on their way back. This could be quite a painful situation for any civilization which claims it to be humanitarian, for a community which is most poor and weak in any socio-economic system. We should not forget that labor communities are the strong pillars of national economy. They have sacrificed their interests through sleepless nights for days, staying without food with kids crying restless, which one fails to express in words. We would win on corona one day or would learn to live with it is as being suggested now by our governments but our corona warriors are going to stay forever, down our memory lane. My salute to corona warriors of the century. Let us pray the Almighty nature to help us out in these hours of risk to human existence on this earth.

*"Prevention is better than cure. When there is no cure then prevention is the only best option. Biodiversity is right now in crisis, rather it should be admitted that the earth itself is in crisis due to biodiversity imbalance. Without balancing of biodiversity humanity cannot survive. Possibilities like the cases of Covid-19 outbreaks cannot be ruled out in future. Salute to the corona warriors. They did all that service to the mankind only on the strength of their willpower, commitment to perform selflessly, generated by their positive mindset to win. Let us pray the Almighty nature to help us."*

----

Lightning Source UK Ltd.
Milton Keynes UK
UKHW011959280622
405105UK00003B/16

9 781543 706963